TAOS
A MEMORY

Miriam Hapgood and Mabel Dodge Luhan.
Yale Collection of American Literature,
Beinecke Rare Book and Manuscript Library,
Yale University.

TAOS

A MEMORY

Miriam Hapgood DeWitt

Introduction by Lois Palken Rudnick

AFTERWORD BY EDWARD BRIGHT

UNIVERSITY OF NEW MEXICO PRESS
Albuquerque

Library of Congress Cataloging-in-Publication Data

DeWitt, Miriam Hapgood, 1906–1990.
Taos: a memory / Miriam Hapgood Dewitt; introduction by
Lois Palken Rudnick; afterword by Edward Bright.—1st ed.
    p.   cm.
Includes bibliographical references.
ISBN 0-8263-1385-X:
1. DeWitt, Miriam Hapgood, 1906–1990.
2. Artists—New Mexico—Taos—Biography.
3. Intellectuals—New Mexico—Taos—Biography.
4. Taos (N.M.)—Social life and customs.
I. Title.
N6537.D4465D48   1992
700'.92—dc20
[B]   92-9670
                                                              CIP

CONTENTS

INTRODUCTION
Lois Palken Rudnick

On June 14, 1983, I sat beside Miriam Hapgood
DeWitt (1906–90) on a small raised platform in the
main hall of the Provincetown Art Association. We
were celebrating another June, in 1915, a germinal
"cultural moment" in American history that saw
the performance of the first two plays written and
produced by the Greenwich Village radicals who
were soon to form the Provincetown Players, a
group of writers and political activists that helped to
lay the foundations for modern American theatre.

Miriam was accompanied by her sister, Beatrix
Hapgood Faust, and by her friends Joel O'Brien and
Heaton Vorse. These four children of the original
founders of the Provincetown Players were present
to bear witness, through their memories and their
parents' memoirs, to the links between the past and
present, for an audience that had come to watch the
restaging of the first two plays by the current Provincetown Playhouse: *Constancy,* by Neith Boyce
Hapgood and *Suppressed Desires* by George (Jig)
Cram Cook and Susan Glaspell. The first play is a
witty spoof of free love, based upon the marriage of
Miriam's parents, Neith and Hutchins Hapgood,

and the love affair between Mabel Dodge and John Reed. The second is a satire of Freudian psychoanalysis. Both plays make wonderful fun of the obsessive tendency of the "young intellectuals" of the prewar era to take each new revolutionary doctrine to heart—whether it be the cry to establish sexual equality through nonmonogamous relationships or the call to "psych" each other's dreams in order to release their pent-up "hidden" selves.[1]

As I listened to Miriam read her father's words about the attempt to create the "Provincetown movement" as "a social effort to live again—spiritually," to recover from their discouragement over the devastation wrought by World War I, I was struck by the connections between our generations.[2] I had interviewed Miriam in March 1983 for my biography of Mabel Dodge Luhan, both because her parents were Mabel's life-long friends and because she had lived in Taos as a friend of Mabel's for thirteen years. But it wasn't until this moment in June 1983 that I *felt* what had driven me to explore the world of her parents' generation. These prewar cultural and political radicals were the "godparents" of my generation of scholar/activists, who grew up in the shadow of Vietnam, another war

1. The plays have been published in *1915: The Cultural Moment: The New Politics, the New Woman, the New Psychology, the New Art, and the New Theatre in America,* ed. Adele Heller and Lois Rudnick (New Brunswick, N.J.: Rutgers University Press, 1991).

2. Hutchins Hapgood, *A Victorian in the Modern World* (New York: Harcourt, Brace and World, 1939), p. 393.

that produced a generation in search of new ways of living and new modes of belief.

The Hapgoods were part of the first generation of Americans to respond to the human costs of our emergence as a major urban industrial power and world empire. Fundamental to their visions of a new America was their belief in the power of individual creative effort to reshape self and society and the power of cultural expression to humanize social life. These early twentieth-century intellectuals, writers, artists, and activists addressed many of the questions that faced my generation in the second half of the century. How do we create a just and democratic society that allows for individual liberty while protecting the collective well-being? How do we establish a socio-economic system that respects individual initiative but also empowers workers, women, and minorities to achieve their fair share of the national wealth that they produce? How do we create a body of art, literature, and cultural criticism that responds to personal vision but also speaks to more than an academic elite and privileged few?

Miriam Hapgood DeWitt grew up in a world where questions like these were part of the meat and drink served at a dinner table that was a "movable feast." In the first decade of the century, her family traveled frequently to Europe, where they befriended the expatriate crowd in Paris at the Gertrude and Leo Stein atelier, and in Florence at the Bernard Berenson villa, I Tatti. In the 1910s they lived in Dobbs Ferry, a suburban enclave for the Greenwich Village bohemians Hutchins worked and played with: Mabel Dodge, Jack Reed, Alfred Stieglitz, Carl Van Vechten, Max Eastman, Lincoln Steffens, and Emma Goldman.

Miriam's parents, Hutchins (1869–1944) and Neith (1872–1951), though much less well known than their more famous peers, are one of the most interesting couples in the annals of twentieth-century American cultural history. They are as worth remembering for their intense and extraordinary life-long devotion to analyzing their relationship as for their individual journalistic and fictional efforts. Hutch, as he was fondly called by his close friends, is the better known of the two. A columnist for the *New York Globe*, he wrote about the sufferings and activities of society's outcasts, both in his columns and a series of books: *The Spirit of the Ghetto* (1902), a remarkably sensitive portrait of the Lower East Side Jewish immigrant community; *The Autobiography of a Thief* (1903); *The Spirit of Labor* (1907); *An Anarchist Woman* (1909); *Types from the City Streets* (1910).

A philosophical anarchist, he supported revolutionary causes of every variety on principle. Yet he was "a Victorian in the modern world," as he appropriately titled his autobiography, who suffered from the feeling that he was a mere "spectator" of life, that he had known only the *forms* of religion, family, and community life. He identified with the ethnic working classes of the ghettoes he frequented because he longed to share what Jane Addams called "the race life." Among the urban poor he found a vitality and sense of community that were lacking in the deracinated world of his mainstream, midwestern, middle-class Protestant boyhood.

It was Hutch who introduced Mabel Dodge to the most interesting members of what became her salon circle. They both embraced the call of the younger generation of rebels in the hope that it would lead to a world in which they could feel at home. Their open-ended commitment to change was paradoxically motivated by a profound yearning for emotional and spiritual certainty—a yearning that was not fulfilled for Mabel until she moved to Taos. They shared what William James had once described to Hutch as a "mad unbridled lust for the absolute," a nineteenth-century disease for which the twentieth century offered no cure. Hapgood's description of the prewar Mabel Dodge in his memoirs is a fair indicator of his own personality—and of the connection between them that would later attract his daughter Miriam to Mabel—and New Mexico:

> Mabel Dodge, as she was then, is the only woman I know who might fairly be called "God-drunk." If at any time she became aware of something just out of reach, she was intensely restless until she had drawn it into her web. She was always talking about "It"; and this was really why Mabel and I understood one another. I have been conscious since my childhood of the unseen cause of all things, which gives to all seen things their superlative beauty; and have been engaged in the hopeless quest of the Cause. . . . I had been on the trail of the Infinite; and still the Infinite torments me. . . . [T]hese desires of hers never sprang from mere curiosity, nor from physical or temperamental whims, though these were frequently obvious elements, but from that indescribable mystic search.[3]

3. Ibid., p. 348.

Neith, who met Hutch while she was the only woman reporter for the New York *Commercial Advertiser*, was also a prolific published writer—of numerous short stories, novels, and plays, mostly about the (unfulfilled) lives of white, middle-class women. Neith grew up in California, where her father cofounded the *Los Angeles Times*. He later moved his family to Boston, where he bought part interest in the *Boston Traveler* and a socialist magazine, *Arena*.

Although her upbringing was much less conventional than Hutch's, including her association with feminists and socialists associated with her father's newspaper in the 1890s, she was the more conservative and emotionally stable element in the marriage. Most of the fiction and plays that Neith wrote about sexual and marital relationships—*The Folly of Others* (1904), *The Eternal Spring* (1906), *Constancy* (1915), *Enemies* (coauthored with Hutch, 1916)—express a skeptical view of the possibility of women and men finding a contented balance between their needs for personal fulfillment and sexual intimacy.[4]

4. Carol Langworthy is editing Neith Boyce's autobiography, which includes an absorbing account of her childhood in California and of her expatriate life in Florence at the turn of the twentieth century. It will be published by the University of New Mexico Press. For an informed analysis of Neith's writing and her marriage to Hutchins see Ellen Kay Trimberger, "The New Woman and the New Sexuality: Conflict and Contradiction in the Writings and Lives of Mabel Dodge and Neith Boyce," in *1915: The Cultural Moment*, ed. Heller and Rudnick, and Trimberger, *Intimate Warriors: Portraits of a Modern Marriage 1899–1940* (New York: Feminist Press, 1991).

Neith's and Hutch's intense struggle over their need to accommodate their individual careers, their marital relationship, and their four children was as much a product of their times and personal politics as it was a matter of temperament. In their attempt to allow each other to experience life and love without jealousy or possessiveness, they were at least in part hoping to live up to the utopian vision of the cultural radicals who believed that the personal could become the political, that their own lives could exemplify the kind of behavior that they promoted in the movements for social and economic justice and equality.

Hutch had been in touch with "free love" anarchists who argued that the marriage contract was part of the property relations of a capitalist society that commodified women. It was mostly his desire, not Neith's, to have affairs with other women in order to live up to his intellectual and emotional commitments never to "crystallize" in life, or love. Neith was much more reluctant than Hutch to experiment successfully and she was terribly hurt by his "experiments." She did fall in love with a mutual friend, for whom she almost left Hutch, suffering in the wake of this relationship a nervous breakdown. In accordance with their group's intriguing tendency to have their art imitate their lives and their lives imitate their art, Hutch wrote, in a privately printed book, an extraordinary and detailed account of their attempts at nonmonogamous marriage, *The Story of a Lover* (1919). It was Neith, however, who recognized the truth that it was typically the woman who suffered in these relationships, and that what the male feminists of her

generation wanted was a wife/mother/mistress/
muse who would serve traditional as well as liberated roles.

Neith's heroine in *Constancy* says to her ex-lover
that his idea of fidelity is to have "a hundred other
women"—and to return to her periodically when in
need of reassurance. Although Hutch did more
than most fathers of his generation in bringing up
his children, Miriam told me that he often criticized
Neith for not devoting enough time to the house,
the children, and their domestic affairs. It was he
who went to his newspaper office in New York City,
while she stayed at home, trying to work, sometimes with the help of servants, but constantly in-
terrupted by the daily affairs of the household.

Miriam also told me that her father was one of
the few men she ever knew in her whole life who
was not "a male chauvinist. I just grew up taking it
for granted that women were the equals of men."
And yet, as her Taos memoir suggests, she was
much less decided than either of her parents about
where she stood in relation to both career and marriage. Given her unconventional parenting, her cosmopolitan education and European travel, one
might expect that Miriam would have had an easier
route to independence and intimate relationships
than her own parents. It is fascinating to speculate
on why this was not so. In fact, one of the most interesting, if subtle, aspects of Miriam's Taos
memoir is the way it illuminates how the roles for
women of her class shifted in the interwar period.

Miriam came of age when the postwar flapper
was all the rage, when as she points out about the
culture shock she experienced when returning from

France to America in 1924, a young woman was judged by her popularity and her "line," not by her intelligence and character.[5] The "new woman" of the 1920s was liberated not in her demand for equality but by her less inhibited social and sexual behavior. Profoundly alienated by this new culture, Miriam shared her father's shocked reaction to the shift in sensibility from Greenwich Village radicalism to the postwar disillusionment of the Jazz Age's "flaming youth." Hutch notes in his autobiography how "the new world to which we came back had thrown over" basic standards of conduct, norms of beauty and art and literature; that the young people he met seemed "languid and bored, even at their drinking parties"; that the speak-easy, night-club, and automobile parties that made up the social life of young people reflected that they "had lost all illusion, they did not love, they merely dissipated."[6]

Neither the Hapgoods' values nor their life-style had prepared Miriam well to deal with this shift in consciousness. Miriam's was an uprooted life, complicated not only by her family's travel and her own parents' ambivalence about family, career, and ambition (Miriam noted to me that her father was never "ambitious" in the traditional way that middle-class men in our culture are expected to be), but also, even if unconsciously, by the emotional stress and complexity of their parents' shifting

5. Miriam's description of dating in the 1920s is an interesting gloss on F. Scott Fitzgerald's short story "Bernice Bobs Her Hair," in *Flappers and Philosophers* (New York: Curtis Publishing Co., 1920).

6. Hapgood, *A Victorian in the Modern World*, p. 495.

sexual/affectional alliances with other men and
women. (Both Miriam and Beatrix claim to have
had no knowledge of their parents' open marriage
practices when they were children, but it is difficult
to believe they were not affected by them.)

Miriam also suffered the fate of many children of
accomplished parents who have to struggle to attain
their own identities under the shadow of their parents' fame, a struggle made more difficult when
their parents have more traditional expectations for
their own children than they did for themselves.
Aside from her short stint at the Elizabeth Duncan
School, Miriam was educated at fairly conservative
boarding schools in America and Europe. In 1928,
she was studying in Paris, at the Sorbonne, on her
junior year abroad from Smith College, when she
became ill, thin, and listless. It is interesting to note
that her father thought the reason for the illness
was that Miriam was "in love with a man without
knowing it, a man she had left in America and later
married."[7]

Miriam tells us that she came to Mabel Luhan's
house in 1929, at a period in her life when she was
suffering from an emotional crisis, although she
does not name that crisis as her husband-to-be Edward Bright. As was true for many visitors who
came there, whether sojourners or permanent set-
tlers, Taos proved to be a healing experience:
Miriam's words suggest that for her it was like a
conversion experience. The battle of wills between
herself and Edward and her parents and Mabel over

7. Ibid., p. 531.

if and when she should marry provides a sometimes amusing and sometimes painful theme in the early years of her memoir. But it becomes increasingly clear, especially after she marries Edward, that he was neither the major cause of—nor the solution to—the malaise and depression she suffered before coming to Taos.

Taos gave Miriam a place and an opportunity to develop her sense of her self and particularly her artist's eye. While she does not seem to have accomplished anything of note in her art during the thirteen years she lived there, she did take up painting seriously for the first time, an occupation that remained a part of her life, in spite of many interruptions, until she died. (None of her work from this period apparently survives. She had showings at the Harwood Gallery in Taos; at the Gallery of Modern Art and other galleries in Washington, D.C.; and at the Provincetown Art Association. Her works are mostly in private collections.) More important for us, her visual and psychological acuity, and her somewhat peripheral position in the Taos art colony as a younger member and lesser light of an extraordinary circle of creative, clashing personalities give her a great advantage as an historian and commentator. This is what makes her book such a delightful contribution to the cultural history of Taos.

Like Joyce Johnson in *Minor Characters*, Miriam looks at Taos "royalty" from the point of view of someone who is a keenly interested but somewhat removed member of that society. It is interesting, first of all, to discover Taos as a refuge from urban-industrial America through the daily life of a more or less ordinary person. There is some nostalgia here, but Miriam romanticizes less than her more famous neighbors and, perhaps because of her own comparative economic marginality, she at least acknowledges the sufferings of the depression in Taos. She treats both the Hispanic and Native American communities with respect and without condescension, although it is clear that her life is lived pretty much within the Anglo enclave.

Miriam's daily life is, of course, enriched by her amusing, pointed, and judicious descriptions and evaluations of the often flamboyant and contentious characters who are part of the Luhan circle, including especially Mabel herself, as well as John Marin, Rebecca Strand, Frieda Lawrence, Dorothy Brett, and Leopold Stokowski. Her memoir is also enriched by the way in which the stories of her life and the world outside Taos interpenetrate her tale. Thus we see Taos both through her eyes and through the wonderful letters from her parents that she incorporates into her text, in the wider framework of writers, journalists, and political activists who exist on the world stage: Hemingway in the early 1920s, as an unassuming young writer and kind friend; Hemingway in the 1930s, as a thrice-married and somewhat dissipated playboy author; a young cousin killed in Spanish Civil War with the Abraham Lincoln Brigade; her sister Beatrix and brother Charles fighting the battles of the left on the side of the Communists and against their "liberal" parents.

During her years in Taos, Miriam was much removed from these political battles. Of all of the Hapgoods, Hutch wrote, Neith and Miriam were

the only ones to eschew leftist politics. In his autobiography, his environmental theory of character
development provides an explanation for this lack
of interest:

> Our daughter Miriam was born within a stone's throw of
> the Santo Spirito bridge over the Arno [in Florence].
> During the months of Neith's pregnancy, the esthetic was
> the predominating thing in our lives; the physical beauty
> of the hills, the pure intense works of art in gallery and
> church, . . . these were daily experiences to the mother,
> surrounded by physical delight, conversational charm and
> gaiety. It is perhaps a fancy only, although I don't think it
> is, that this child born of our union has always seemed to
> us Florentine; . . . Since her childhood, too, this girl has
> shown a continuous esthetic interest and plastic gift, ex-
> quisite in feeling and touch, corresponding to the quality
> of her physical being, of a femininity that goes beyond
> femaleness, seemingly an enhancement created by the
> master's touch.[8]

Whatever truth there is in his theory, Hutch's
loving description of his first-born daughter helps
to account for the pleasure the reader of her memoir will take in her verbal gifts. He would have
been equally pleased to discover that she developed
other interests after his death that suggest the staying power of the Hapgood family's seeming pre-
disposition to political activism. Edward Bright, her
son, describes this part of her career in his afterword to this book.

Taos: A Memory leaves us with the vivid impressions of the thirteen-year period when Miriam
most strongly cultivated her aesthetic disposition,

8. Ibid., p. 228.

told from a perspective of an eighty-four-year-old woman who was as fully awake in all of her senses when she wrote it as when she was brought back to life during her first visit to New Mexico:

> The fall and winter are almost too beautiful—like a pang. The roadsides are alight with massed sunflowers, the aspens are yellow patterns on the mountainside, the cottonwoods in the valley a deep gold. Colors deepen in the lowering light. The first snow descends in a cloud on Taos mountain, the air is like strong drink. To be alive is exciting.

TAOS
A MEMORY

"We are in the maddest, most amusing country in the world—in the freakiest most insane village you ever dreamed of and I would like to stay forever! . . You'd better come out here!"
Mabel Dodge, in a letter to Neith Hapgood, 1918.

It is now the summer of 1929. We get off the train at Lamy—Mother, my brother Charles, and I. It is the stop for Santa Fe, the capital of New Mexico, yet there is only a small station surrounded by desert. The astringent odor of sagebrush is strong in the hot sun. Spud Johnson, writer, printer and publisher of a literary magazine, the *Laughing Horse*, is there to meet us in Mabel's open car. We drive through the ancient Spanish city, then start out on the road to Taos, seventy-five rugged miles away.

I have lived three years in western Europe, seen the Alps, but have never been west of New York state. My response to the strange country is immediate. For two years I have been in what I suppose is a state of depression, not myself my parents say, no life in me. The brilliant sun, the clear dry air, the unearthly red rock hills rolling away to mountains, the space—they affect me like a conversion. I know it is where I want to live.

The road is unpaved and narrow. Arroyos, gullies through which mud-gorged waters pour after a thunderstorm in the mountains, are sometimes impassable. We encounter short local storms, black clouds release their torrents, the road is muddy but we are able to continue. We descend from 7,000 feet at Santa Fe to about 5,000 at the level of the Rio Grande, a small river here flowing through a valley of orchards and vegetable gardens. Then begins the long climb up again around hairpin turns that slice the rocky walls of the river's deep canyon and leave the sparkling river far beneath.

Suddenly, Taos Valley spreads out before us, slightly rolling, dotted with piñon and cedar in the higher places, mostly sagebrush. Away to the right and left are distant mountain ranges, before us is Taos Mountain, still a few miles away, but dominant and enfolding, an ancient, rounded, benevolent presence, now aglow in the late sun.

We drive through the old village of Ranchos de Taos, past the impressive adobe church, across a few more miles of empty sagebrush desert, through Taos's dusty plaza, where a few horses and wagons are hitched to rails, on up a narrow dirt lane and we are there! To one side of a small courtyard is the gate to Mabel's "Big House," always called that although officially its name is "Los Gallos," the chickens, after a row of large ceramic fowl along the top of the *portal*. To the other side is the gate to the Santa Theresa house, where we are to stay as Mabel's guests. Mabel Dodge Luhan has been a friend of my parents since 1913 when she moved to New York from Italy and soon afterward started her famous salon at 23 Fifth Avenue. There the movers and shakers of the time—artists and writers, liberals and anarchists, labor leaders—came together to talk. But in 1917 she was to discover Taos, meet her Indian husband, Tony, and settle there.

I have never seen anything like it. The house is built of adobe, local earth mixed with straw, as are all Mabel's houses and most others in Taos. The walls, window and door openings and the fireplaces, molded by Indian women, show the touch of their bare hands. The beams of the ceiling are peeled trees; across them are laid saplings in a straight or herringbone pattern. The walls are painted with a white earth, tierra blanca, applied with a sheepskin; tiny bits of mica embedded in the earth reflect the light. At the St. Theresa house we enter the living-room. Under the very large paned window is a big day-bed covered by an embroidered spread and numerous cushions all in gay colors. A tin cage containing a large wooden parrot hangs near it and a Mexican tin chandelier for candles is suspended in the center of the room. The pine floors are covered with Indian blankets. On the walls are Mexican embroideries, Indian paintings, tin mirrors and a santo or two. The chairs are of wood covered with hide or brightly painted. There are a few old chests of Spanish Colonial design. All is lively, simple, comfortable and charming.

My brother, Charles, put well our feelings about our new surroundings in his first letter home to my father: "This country seems to me like the other side of the moon, nature being so different from anything I have ever imagined before that the similarities to my former way of living stand out in isolation, like a few scattered known words in a strange language."

Mabel had invited some young people for the summer, including me, my brother Charles and Charles Collier, son of the Commissioner of Indian

Affairs. The plan did not include Mother, who did not want to go, preferring to stay home with her husband, her younger daughter, her garden and her writing. But suddenly, Mabel had to go off to Buffalo for an operation and Mother felt she had to be there with us at the first. This was tragic country for her. Her eldest child, a son, Boyce, had died alone in Dawson, not very far away, during the influenza epidemic of 1918. She had been on her way to him by train but was too late to see him alive.

The morning after our arrival Charles and I find our way to the kitchen of the Big House where we are to have breakfast. Maria is standing at the big range. Two parrots in separate cages are chatting in an undertone. At one end of the room near a window facing east on sagebrush two women sit at a blue oilcloth-covered table. We are introduced to Georgia O'Keeffe and Rebecca Strand. They are about the same height and build and dressed alike in black skirts and white shirts. Georgia's black hair is pulled straight back to a knot. Becky's, prematurely gray, parted in the middle, frames her madonna-like face.

"Ah! Ella," Georgia says, as another woman appears at the door. "You were up very early. I saw you passing my window."

"No, you must have seen my astral body."

It is Ella Young, the Irish mystic and writer. She is a strangely attractive figure. Draped in loose buckskin, a blue scarf tied about her wispy white hair, her eyes wide and innocent, she could be a character out of one of her own Irish tales.

After breakfast I walk across to the Pink House where Georgia and Becky are staying. It is small with a wooden porch overlooking the alfalfa field that supplies some of the fodder for Mabel's and Tony's horses. The alfalfa is in purple bloom and filled with bees. The Big House and St. Theresa House top the rise where the lane comes up from the road. At that level the acequia madre, or mother ditch, bringing irrigation water from Blue Lake hidden far up Taos Mountain to smaller ditches and thus to fields and gardens, flows between the Big House and the alfalfa field sloping toward the Pink House. Cottonwood, willow, wild olive cluster on the banks. A bridge in front of the Big House, which widens to accommodate two old-fashioned gliders, or hanging sofas, leads to a board walk across the field. Behind the Pink House is the two-story house where John Marin, his wife and son are staying. Nearby is the studio Georgia is using. She is painting Ranchos church. Sometimes when I visit her there she is sewing white linen shirts for her husband, Alfred Stieglitz, who is far away in Lake George. Her stitches are precise and even and beautiful as her brush strokes. Her house in Abiquiu, in the red-rock country north of Santa Fe, where she will eventually settle, is all-of-a-piece with her painting: simple, flowing lines, select stones from the Colorado River in the courtyard, a few choice paintings, a snake's skeleton under glass.

Becky's husband, Paul, a photographer, member of the Stieglitz group of artists, is also in the East. Becky is painting exquisite flowers on glass. It is a technique, but not a style, she has borrowed from the Victorians. The paint is applied to the back of the glass so that the painting process is reversed, with the highlights applied first. It is a painstaking and finicky process, yet some of her effects are quite bold and free. Her "Portrait of Miriam—1929," a sunflower in a blue vase, reflects the transformation that was taking place in me that summer.

Becky is the daughter of Nate Salsbury, who founded the "Wild West Show," traveling with Barnum and Bailey's circus and Buffalo Bill, and of a proper Victorian lady who wore lace mitts. Outwardly she is her father's daughter. She dresses in pants, a black Stetson, her shirt carelessly open, a cigarette always dangling from a corner of her mouth. She rides her horse to a lather, talks tough, associates with the gamblers and rough characters of the town, John Dunn, Doughbelly Price, Bing Abbott—figures out of the old West. Yet enter her house—she later moved to Taos and lived there many years—and you are in a precisely ordered, almost lace-doilied world.

At dinner in the Big House we are to meet the Marins. We approach the front door through big gates, pass a row of pigeon houses on poles high up among the branches of the cottonwoods, cross a large courtyard and enter on a *portal*, a covered walkway supported by posts and carved corbels. On the long wall of the house is a painting of an Indian performing the Eagle dance. Big, heavy, double doors that open at the top lead into the living room. The many beautiful things in this room reflect Mabel's past and present. A large carved and gilded Buddha over the fireplace, on the mantel a row of beautifully carved ivory skulls and two or three memento mori boxes like tiny coffins (in which, Mabel says, the offending member of his wife's lover was sent to her) are from her villa in Italy.

There are a large carved dresser, French upholstered chairs, some of the paintings from her New York salon days and many by Taos artists. On the floor are fine Navajo rugs. In a far corner is a square high-sided couch from her New York apartment where she retires from company from time to time "to go into the silence" as she puts it. All the elements combine into a dignified, inviting, restful whole.

Spud is there as host. It is Prohibition and he mixes cocktails—orange juice and "Taos Lightning," raw corn whiskey. We have a fire in the adobe fireplace, for when the sun goes down summer evenings are often cool. The burning piñon sends out an aromatic smell. Vases of fresh flowers add their perfume to the pleasant underlying odor of waxed furniture.

The dining room is down several steps to the kitchen level. Albidia of the sad and beautiful face is serving, moving silently in her folded white buckskin boots. It is said that she has an unrequited passion for Mabel's handsome son, John, but is married to Manuel, the master carver whose leaves and flowers are on all the doors in the house, who made Mabel's bed with its carved spiral posts and painted the mural of the *portal*. The bronze bust over the main gate, the work of Maurice Sterne, is a portrait of Albidia.

Marin is small, wiry, with fuzzy bobbed hair, an expressive face, sparkling black eyes and a sense of humor. His wife appears motherly and pleasant; his son is fourteen and silent; the simple food is good. The talk is about a spectacular murder that has just been discovered: John Manby, Mabel's landlord when she and Maurice Sterne first came to Taos, has been found with his head severed and chewed by his two fierce guard dogs. He was an English remittance man—that is, paid to stay out of England lest he disgrace his family. Locally he has been involved in shady mining deals. Suspects are named; there is a long trial, which everyone attends; but nothing can be proved. Some think the dogs have killed him.

Mother is feeling the altitude and not going about much, but Charles and I fall right into the life. We go on pack trips of several days each up Taos Mountain, the Indians' sacred mountain. At its foot stands Taos Pueblo; lakes are hidden in its folds; the Pueblo river flows out of it; it abounds in game. Some of the Pueblo's most secret ceremonials are held there. We are prepared for romance and we find it—Georgia O'Keeffe, Charles Collier, two Indian guides, Tony and Jim Mirabal, Charles and I—on horseback with an extra horse or two to carry our food and sleeping bags. In a letter to our father, my brother gives a good account of our experiences.

"Our first trip of four days took us up through the great canyon on the other side of Taos Mountain, the walls of which canyon are at times a thousand feet high. The canyon is about fourteen miles long, with a crystal torrent rushing through it and heavy timber growing to some height. We passed through great groves of aspens, 150 feet high, looking like thousands of white columns in some Arabian nights' palace. We climbed out of the ravine into a valley more than two miles above sea level. The slopes around it were in places covered with snow. The lower end was forested and a deep blue lake occupied the center. We swam in the lake though it was ice cold. I had the surprising experience of walking barefoot over snow drifts four feet deep the sun at the same time blistering my back . . . The whole valley, the deep ravines and the mountain sides were just plastered with wild flowers. The tops to which we climbed were just blue and gold with forget-me-nots and buttercups, and the fragrance of the flowers filled the air like incense. We saw dozens and dozens of varieties, including violets and roses and anemones and wild columbine and wild larkspur, blue gentian, daisies of all kinds, giant dandelions, great masses of lilies and flowering grasses, and all of them intensely fragrant."

It rains every afternoon for a short time, cooling the air, so that it is very cold at night—sometimes so cold that Georgia and I share the same sleeping bag. We have fresh trout for breakfast and in the evening sit around a campfire while the Mirabals beat their drums and chant their Indian melodies. They are intelligent, interesting men, who know a lot about Indian affairs and the world outside the pueblo.

Charles continues: "On our way back from this camping ground we climbed the peak of Mt. Wheeler (14,000 feet) and glimpsed all the kingdoms of the earth, in Biblical fashion, so to speak. We walked the horses along ridges that made one actually dizzy—for one could see almost perpendicular slopes on every hand descending a thousand feet or more."

Some way short of the peak, I develop a charley

horse and am forced to stay behind. A short, sharp thunderstorm drives me under a projecting rock. When the others return they look wan and dishevelled. Sheet lightning has knocked off Charles's hat, his hair stands on end and they are all scared. We leave the peak as quickly as possible and take another route home.

I am impressed by our horses—just ordinary western ponies—but intelligent and capable. They stand when the reins are trailing the ground, they know how to get over and around fallen trees and rocks, they never step false, they seem tireless and they eat whatever is available wherever they are.

A week or so later we go out again, for six days this time but not so deep into the mountain. "Our narrow path followed," Charles writes, "the course of a swift stream. We occasionally found deserted bear traps and here as elsewhere came across cattle, horses and sheep turned loose. We camped at night on a friend's ranch, where the girls (Miriam and Georgia) slept inside. But the inside was very public as the girls were awakened every night by wild animals. Chipmunks entered the kitchen (kitchen and bedroom are virtually one) and knocked down pans, etc. One night a coyote entered the kitchen, or at least howled just outside the girls' window, terrifying them. Night before last an enormous porcupine entered their bedroom and had to be ejected by force." I almost step on it getting out of bed in the dark.

The friend's ranch is the place on Lobo mountain that Mabel traded to D. H. Lawrence in exchange for the manuscript of Sons and Lovers. The Lawrences are in France, where he is very ill with tuberculosis. Brett is living at the ranch for the summer. She was born the Honorable Dorothy Brett, daughter of Viscount Esher, who was a significant figure at the courts of Victoria and Edward VII. At Buckingham Palace she attended dancing school to which the old Queen sometimes lent her presence, terrifying the children by pounding on the floor with her heavy cane when she was displeased. Brett broke away from her aristocratic roots when she attended the Slade art school and became a serious painter. In London she met the Lawrences, became obsessed by D. H., followed him to Taos and lived there for the rest of her life. When I meet her she must be in her forties. She is plumpish but sturdy and very active, with a round face, pink cheeks, rather beautiful brown eyes full of mischief, buck teeth and short bobbed hair. She wears baggy velveteen pants, a beaded leather vest, boots and a Stetson. She is very deaf and carries "Toby," an ear trumpet that looks like some primitive musical instrument—a long tube flaring into a circular flat pan-like piece open at the end which somewhat resembles an ash tray. She points it at the speaker; sometimes, at parties, people jokingly deposit their ashes in the pan. She has her own very English but unique brand of humor and is fun to be with. On a very small income from her family in England, she manages a good life. She travels alone in her station wagon or with some of her Indian friends to ceremonials far and wide. Many of these she has painted from memory, for sketching or photographing at the scene are forbidden. She seems to me one of the few painters to catch the spirit and beauty of Indian life. Part of the year she lives in Mabel's

studio—the one Georgia is now using. She is one
of the regulars, along with Spud and later Myron
[Brinig], so we are often together of an evening at
Mabel's. Every now and then she and Mabel quarrel and there is a rift for a while, but eventually
they make up.

In her book, *Lawrence and Brett*, published in
1933, in a series of vignettes, Brett paints a picture
of daily life on the Lawrence ranch with Lawrence
and Frieda: of riding down the mountain to the
neighboring Hawk ranch for milk; then Lawrence
milking their own cow, angry with it for playing
hide and seek among the trees; angrily wringing
the neck of a broody hen; felling trees and chop-
ping wood for the stove; baking bread in an out-
door adobe oven; building a porch; Brett always
adoring, protecting, helping, always siding with
Lawrence in his arguments with Frieda; Frieda
lying on her bed smoking or cooking, angry with
Lawrence for acting the master when, she says, she
was the master back at her baronial home in Germany. She is fed up with Brett's worship of her
husband, finally banning her from the place except
when explicitly invited—Brett must signal her approach by blowing a whistle. Lawrence and Brett
paint together. He compares her work unfavorably
with his own. The book gives the impression that
Lawrence used Brett as a convenience and buffer
between him and Frieda and her rages. I think he
enjoyed having two high-born women more or less
subject to him, the son of a miner. Nevertheless,
that he enjoyed Brett's company and was fond of
her is apparent in the last scene in Brett's book
when he goes to see her in Capri after a fight with

Frieda. It is a sad scene, for she returns to America and the ranch and never sees him again. After Lawrence dies, Frieda returns to the ranch with her Italian lover, Angelino Ravagli, a captain in a crack regiment, the Bersaglieri. I remember having seen, in Florence, the romantic uniform of this regiment, the helmets embellished with a cascade of iridescent cock feathers. "Angy" is a friendly, simple man who, he says, thought he was a "great man" until he left Italy and found out that Lawrence was famous. Frieda is big, blonde, hearty and hospitable, with a pot au feu as hearty as she is, containing whole onions, tomatoes, carrots and potatoes, on the back of the stove. She and Brett, who builds her own cabin about a mile away, remain friendly enemies.

Often during that summer I go out with the Marin family to paint usually in the mountains or foothills where there is a fast-running stream. Marin seems fascinated by the movement of water. His palette always looks a brownish mess, yet out of it emerges his clear vibrant color. I am also painting in watercolor and of course am heavily influenced by his style. That amuses him. According to a letter from Mabel to Mother, he jokes that he will send one of my paintings along with his to Stieglitz! The following winter I visit the Marins for a day at their home in New Jersey. I am surprised for it seems drab and ordinary. The furniture and rugs are dark brown. None of his sparkle and lightness of spirit come through to his surroundings.

While Charles and I are in heaven, poor Mother is miserable. Her letters to Father form a sort of counterpoint to our raptures. She does not feel well; the altitude has affected her heart. Where we see only beauty and romance, she sees poverty and disease and danger. She has a touch of malaria; a nest of rattlesnakes is discovered under our doorstep. "I don't like this country," she writes, "too many queer things here . . . Marin is sweet and his pictures are the only ones that even suggest this crazy country . . . Poor O'Keeffe loves it here but Stieglitz keeps writing and telegraphing her to come back to him! . . She says she hates Lake George and all his family." Mother enjoys the beauty and likes the Indians but hates everything else about the place. "It is nice to see Tony here at home. He moves in this atmosphere with grace and dignity—busy with affairs of the place and Pueblo." He is worried and nervous over Mabel's operation. "They are evidently very close together."

In a letter to my sister, Beatrix, she describes a corn dance we attend: "We have just come back from a two-day trip with Tony to see a dance in an Indian town. We drove to Santa Fe, stayed overnight at a funny place called Hotel El Fidel (The Faithful Hotel!) and next morning drove through wonderful desert country to the Indian town. It was terribly hot but interesting. All the Indians were dressed in their best, brilliant orange, green, purple, with heaps of silver and turquoise jewelry. The dance began about 2 o'clock and lasted till 7 P.M. The dancers, men, women and children, were naked to the waist and painted either brown or blue—in fact they wore nothing except elaborate headdresses and girdles of green pine branches, fox-furs and beads. How they kept it up in the hot sun, singing, dancing, and beating drums, I don't know—some were old too, men and women. The whole place was a riot of color. The governor of the town, a wizened old Indian, had cerise trousers and purple shirt, and he rushed around keeping a vicious eye on the white people and jumped on a woman who had a camera as it is forbidden to take pictures of the dance—it being a sacred affair designed to make the corn grow and to bring rain . . . We were quite exhausted when we got back to Santa Fe and stayed overnight again at El Fidel. I have often wished you were with us. You would enjoy the horses and expeditions to the mountains."

Mother intends leaving soon after Mabel's return in early August. Her trunk goes down on the last stage to leave for Santa Fe in a week, as heavy rains wash out the road. In any case, she cannot leave until things quiet down. "Everything is upset since Mabel got back and everybody quarreling!" she writes her husband. "I can't leave the children to keep things straight with Mabel! She of course isn't feeling well and is nervous and irritable and we, alas, are in the same house with her and the other house is torn up putting in a furnace, so we have to stay here and it's like walking on eggs! . . . Well, so far it's been nice here. How it will be now I don't know—but must wait and see. You remember I told you we'd have trouble!" A few days later: "The trouble here is that Mabel isn't strong and yet she insisted on rushing around to all her houses and trying to run everything and tell us all what we should do, and she got very irritated and over-did and now she is in bed with her heart not working right. There are a number of people here whom she had invited, including us, but now it's too much for her and she has quarreled with them all except me and she has quarreled with them all except me and tried to quarrel with me, but I wouldn't! I real-ize that she has undertaken too much in having people here, as she is apt to do. She invites and then gets fed up with them! Yet I know she doesn't want us to go, or I would leave in a minute—but it is just going to take a lot of diplomacy to get along. . . .

"An amusing complication is Georgia O'Keeffe. She was very nice until Mabel got back. But she is an awful egotist and has to be the most important person. So she left, taking Charles C. with her to drive her car and has kept him away ever since—has just taken him on a two-weeks trip to Grand Canyon; though he didn't want to go she abso-lutely bullied him into it! He was very devoted to Miriam—here all the time—and is gay and amus-ing, so he and our two had a very good time to-gether. And as there are no other young people here I am sorry for his abduction!

"Mabel said to Georgia, 'I don't think you'd bet-ter try to get Charles away, as he will have a much better time here with young people of his own age!' And Georgia said, 'Well, I am going to make him go!' Miriam wouldn't say a word to get him to stay, so he went, looking like a poor little rabbit! So Mabel is furious at Georgia! There are a lot of other squabbles but I won't go into them now."

Mabel's heart gives out and she goes into the hospital in Albuquerque. She doesn't speak to Mother before she leaves and so Mother is puzzled as to whether she doesn't want us all to clear out. "She has so often invited people and then thrown them out that I seem to recognize the symptoms."

But Charles and I don't want to go and in the end
Mabel calms down, Mother goes home, Charles and
I stay and all is well. Charles writes Mabel about a
ghost he has seen. Ghosts are not new to Mabel;
her villa in Florence was haunted. Mother was
driven out by the ghostly presence when she visited
Mabel there in 1914. Mabel replies from the hospital: "I was thrilled by your letter and only hope we
have a nice gentle ghost there. I wouldn't mind at
all if it isn't a mean or disagreeably horrific ghost.
When you go of course Miriam must move over to
the big house to one of the bedrooms by the bath
room. I don't know if I will be back by September
4. . . . Write me at once if any more happens about
the ghost."

My health is one reason we have accepted
Mabel's invitation to come to Taos. Toward the
close of my junior year at Smith College when,
with a group from my class, I was studying at the
Sorbonne in Paris, living with a French family, I
was ailing. Perhaps reason enough was the rainy
climate, sitting long hours on cold stone benches, or
the rich food; but the family doctor was called in
and raised the specter of t.b., still at the time a
dread disease. When a cable was sent, Father, always a worrier, whom Lincoln Steffens called "the
mother of the family," took the next boat for
France. Although a specialist ruled out t.b., he
whisked me out of Paris to the Haute-Savoie,
stuffed me with *petits pains,* honey and jam. I must
gain weight. After a week or so I felt like a goose
being fattened for *pâté de foie gras.* My father had
always tended to be overprotective of his children,
but since my brother's death he was morbidly so.

Even though we were especially close and he did his best to make life pleasant for me, his obsession with my health was becoming a burden; it was like being covered with a heavy blanket.

My indisposition became a depression. According to my parents letters, my personality changed; I lost my energy and *joie de vivre*. Even today I do not understand what happened to me, what was the cause of the depression, nor why it vanished suddenly in Taos. Perhaps I needed to get away from home; perhaps it was the interruption of my college plans and sudden severing of that connection; perhaps that intensified the feeling of not belonging that had lingered since my return from two years in France in 1924.

The French culture of the time was very different from the American of the "Roaring Twenties." During the summer of 1923 in Provence when I was sixteen, I had had my first thrilling taste of male attention; two French boys were rivals for my favor. But I was surrounded by family and friends and French custom imposed strict guardianship of a *jeune fille*. Not even a kiss was exchanged. The sexual hurricane had not yet swept the Continent. When I returned to the United States I was not in any way prepared for the craziness of the Prohibition era in America. It was the time of speakeasies, pocket flasks, heavy drinking among the young, coonskin coats, stag lines and ruthless competition for popularity. Unless you were rushed off your feet at dances by men "cutting in," you were unpopular, a failure. The pack of stags, close together, flasks on hip, formidable, looked you over, watched to see how many others cut in. If you were popular, you were rushed to death; if not, you were "stuck" and humiliated. Sometimes a boy who was "stuck" would hold out a bribe behind the poor girl's back. The aim of most young women was to accumulate as many "beaus" as possible. It was the number of scalps that counted. Unsophisticated, unsure, terrified, I was suddenly confronted with an alien world. When I could invent a string of improbable lies, known as a "line," I had a few wild successes at parties; at others I had humiliating failures. As I look back, I can see how brutal the system was and how shallow the prevailing attitudes but at the time I was trying to conform—to somehow fit into this new world where flippancy and craziness were the sought-for qualities. I had admirers, but I never felt sure of myself, never at ease with boys. In college, too, the girls I knew were caught up in the same frenzied culture and were mostly concerned with weekend dates, proms and clothes. Although college work was interesting, sometimes exciting, marriage occupied our thoughts of the future; it offered the surest way to "independence" open to most women even then.

The summer after my return from my earlier sojourn in France, in 1925, I met a man at the house of a friend in Orleans on Cape Cod, and began a relationship that was to be of great importance in my life. (To my emotional conflict over him, my parents were later to attribute my depression.) We were all on our way to a costume ball in Provincetown. I was wearing a very becoming dress I had made of white kitchen oilcloth, long and off the shoulder. Edward fell in love with me on the spot. I spent the next five years trying to make up my mind how I felt about him. I was eighteen, he was twelve years older, had been a pilot in the Lafayette Escadrille, then an ambulance driver after we entered the war. He flew gliders off the cliffs at Highland Light in Truro. He had lived most of his life abroad, he was very tall and slim and had an air about him, he was silent, rather withdrawn. There was romance somehow; perhaps it was his very difference from the other boys I knew. He didn't take part in the fun at parties; he didn't fit in, and this bothered me. We broke it off several times; then he would turn up and it would start again. One time I was taking a walk along the road and he happened to pass by though he lived with his parents in Sandwich at the other end of the Cape. Another time I was at the station in FitzWilliam, New Hampshire, near my mother's farm, meeting a friend, when his face appeared in the train window. Fate seemed determined to bring us together.

My parents were glad when, in 1927, I put an ocean between us, for they felt a lack of life force in him. I had other admirers during those years, beaus we called them; we necked and petted; but few girls went further than that. I did not fall seriously in love; my thoughts kept returning to Edward; he wrote to me in Paris; he was always there in the background waiting.

After the abrupt ending of my college year and my return to America, instead of making up the work and returning to Smith, I spent a foolish winter in New York, going to speakeasies and parties. I was deeply unsatisfied, directionless; I did not belong; my feelings were confused; Edward was sometimes in the picture, sometimes not. Then came Taos, and the wonder of it all crowded him into the background of my thoughts.

After Mother returns to Richmond, Mabel takes over the care of Charles and me. She evidently likes having us around—we had been well trained to be polite and considerate of our elders. Charles goes back to college in September while, at Mabel's invitation, I stay on into winter. The fall and winter are almost too beautiful—like a pang. The roadsides are alight with massed sunflowers, the aspens are yellow patterns on the mountainside, the cottonwoods in the valley a deep gold. Colors deepen in the lowering light. The first snow descends in a cloud on Taos mountain, the air is like strong drink. To be alive is exciting. From the roof of the house I do many paintings of the mountain. I am exhilarated by the grandeur of the place. I enjoy the company of Mabel, Tony and their friends; it is the beginning of a long and unbroken friendship. Mabel and Tony and I often ride together, usually into the low hills behind the Big House. Sometimes I am mounted on Tony's pinto stallion—so different in spirit from the horses or even my little mare. Tony is like a bronze equestrian statue, his red and blue chief's blanket wrapped around him, a massive figure at one with his horse. His broad handsome face is framed by braids bound in purple and white tape. He moves with measured dignity. When he laughs or jokes the tranquil, rather stern lines of his face break apart, his eyes become triangular, he looks boyish.

Mabel, too, sits her horse well. She is stocky, her black hair cut in a bang like the Indian women, a scarf around her head. At this period of her life her face and figure are undistinguished and she wears simple dresses with gathered skirts. But her extraordinary eyes, hazel and thickly lashed, her deep, beautifully modulated voice and her self-assurance set her apart. They demand attention and respect. Yet it is difficult to explain her power. She is not at all beautiful, nor charming, nor very warm. She is not witty, nor particularly intellectual, though very intelligent, observant and intuitive. Nor is she, so far as I know, especially knowledgeable, except in a general way as the result of her varied life experience. She has a strong will and knows what she wants and does not want at any given time. Money, generosity and beautiful surroundings make her invitations attractive, but that does not explain why D. H. Lawrence, Robinson Jeffers, Leopold Stokowski and many other men and women of distinction come and come again. She has a mysterious power to attract, to stimulate, to bring people together. Lincoln Steffens called it her "centralizing, magnetic, social faculty." He said that men like to sit with her and talk to themselves. It is easy to see why some people are her friends and why many are her enemies. To those she has taken into her close circle she is warm, hospitable, concerned with their problems, companionable and fun. To those she doesn't take to or who bore her—often for no good reason—she can be cold, arrogant and rude. She can suddenly turn on those she has invited or befriended. This is one reason for her usual bad press. Another is that in her *Intimate Memories,* as my father says in his autobiography, she tends to focus on her worst side. I see mostly the Mabel of her book *Winter in Taos,* an account of her daily life with Tony. In this lovely book she emerges as sensitive, and observant of the life around her—of nature, of animals, of farming, of the Mexicans in the surrounding villages, especially of daily life in the Pueblo. It is a tender picture of the ordinary inhabitants of Taos Valley, her kinship with them and her relationship with her Indian husband. Through Tony and the Indians, Mabel has achieved a sense of "broad, deep life."

Often we go on long drives, sometimes through the abandoned mining towns of Red River and Elizabethtown in the mountains, sometimes up to the Lobo or to Arroyo Hondo and other small towns in the valley. In the evenings we sit around the fragrant fire of piñon, play mah-jongg, consult the I Ching, read detective stories or gossip with Brett and Spud. Or we play records in the rainbow room—so called for its ceiling painted in rainbow colors one day by artist friends. Or we help Mabel sew rings on curtains, all of which she makes herself. There are always new books from the lending library in Santa Fe, there are blooming plants or bowls of fresh flowers, their fragrance mingles with the aromatic smoke of cedar twigs wafted about the room as Mabel lights and then blows them out.

Sometimes in the late afternoon Mabel will say, "Come on, Miriam, let's go to the pueblo." We park on the bridge over the river that flows between the two main buildings. Silent, we listen to the river and the sounds of Indian life, the governor calling out instructions from the top of one of the two many-storied buildings, the men coming in from the fields where grain is being threshed and winnowed. In the fields outside the pueblo we see them throwing the oats into the air where the wind blows away the chaff and the grain falls onto the packed earth.

With end of summer the cast of characters has changed. Georgia and Becky and Charles Collier have gone. Ella Young is in the Pink House. The Marins have gone and Andrew Dasburg and Nancy Lane, his pretty new wife, are honeymooning in the St. Theresa house, spending most of their days trout fishing in the mountain streams. Nancy, the daughter of Wilson's Secretary of Interior, is Andrew's second or third wife. In a few years he will divorce her and marry Owen Wister's daughter, Marina, and settle in Ranchos de Taos. There, after divorcing her, he will spend the rest of his long life. Andrew is an old and close friend of Mabel from New York days. He is handsome and winning and a fine artist who continues painting and drawing well into his eighties.

Ella Young and I become friends. We go out for a "gallup" every day and I see her home to the Pink House after dinner and light her fire. She tells me about her life in Ireland where she was a member of the literary circle including Yeats and where she drove a team of snow-white mules through the streets of Dublin. She has published several books of fairy tales and will go on to Berkeley where, I am told, a chair of mythology has been created for her.

Spud is away and Ernie O'Malley is staying in his house. He is writing a book about the Irish war of independence. He entered the rebel army at nineteen, was a brigadier general at twenty-one, has eight bullets in his back, was captured by the

British, tried to pass as a farmer, but was betrayed by his small uncalloused hands—he had actually been in medical school—and tortured. Red-hot pokers were held near his eyes, his eyesight permanently damaged; he wears thick glasses. He is a romantic figure.

When the weather turns cold Brett will move from the Lobo into Georgia's studio but now she has an unwelcome guest—Georgia's sister, Ida. According to Brett, Ida practiced black magic in a previous incarnation. She scares away the nature spirits and spirits of the mountain that Brett has called forth around her. She fears everything. Everett Marcy, an attractive young friend, and I visit the ranch one night and find Ida in her cabin with a loaded automatic. She is jealous of Georgia, says she would have been a much better painter.

Marcy and I are good friends, nothing more, but Mabel gets the wind up and, unbeknownst to me, writes my parents. She is often perceptive in her analysis of people and situations, but often wrong. Although my parents have had experience with Mabel and know her failings, they are all stirred up. Mother responds: "I should be very reluctant to interfere between her and another man, for the reason that I think our attitude did influence her very much in that other love-affair which had such a bad effect on her and perhaps made her really give the man [Edward] up—for she is very susceptible to the attitude of certain people. Hutch has always influenced her a lot and I suppose I have. One reason I left her out there was my feeling that she must begin to decide things for herself and shape her own life—even if she makes a temporary mess of it! . . But even if there is danger of her falling in love seriously when Marcy isn't serious or is a bad bet, I think the danger of trying to break it off would be greater and I'm in favor of letting her settle it all herself. She will have to face life for herself anyway. No one can really protect her except at the risk of making her helpless for living which I think is the worst fate."

The flap soon ends as Marcy leaves for California. Tony and I drive him to the airport—to fly at that time is still an adventure. On the way home between Santa Fe and Taos we spend the night along with about one hundred others when we are unable to cross a storm-swollen arroyo.

San Geronimo day, September 30, marks the end of summer. Geronimo is the Christian saint who presides over the Indians' ancient harvest celebrations. The pueblo is newly washed, cracks sealed with liquid mud, and gay with multicolored corn piled high on platforms. Indians in their bright shirts and dresses are clustered on all levels of the tall buildings. On a track beside the river young men are running, old men in white buckskin are urging them on with cries and a rhythmic beating of the air with branches of yellow aspen. It is one of the most beautiful of the ceremonies, the white and gold, the red, green and black-painted bodies of the runners against the dark blue towering Sacred Mountain. It is a relay race between the two sides of the pueblo but the object is not to win. It is in some way to honor the earth for its bounty and to prepare it for the winter's sleep. Soon shoes will be removed from the horses, cars and wagons put up until spring lest they disturb its rest.

A tall pine trunk, peeled and greased, a sheep carcass and other prizes tied to its summit, stands in the big open space, or plaza, between the two main buildings. Koshare, their bodies painted white, a top-knot of corn stalks in their white painted hair, will attempt to climb the slippery pole. They are the clowns or fools; in pantomime they mock the tourists; in the afternoon they play a comic part in the last corn dance of the season.

San Geronimo is also a festival day for the town. In the evening we go to a ball and to John Dunn's gambling den on the plaza. There we can play roulette, blackjack and other games; only a bead curtain separates the gamblers from the street. "Long John Dunn," reputed to be a murderer who long ago fled the law to New Mexico, then a territory, drives the stage from Taos to Santa Fe. He is one of the remnants of the wide-open frontier—a figure out of the Old West in attitude and speech and dress. The old timers, along with more recent arrivals are, in general, classified as "Anglos" to distinguish them from the Indians and "Mexicans." Some of the old-timers are artists; many have lived here since the 1890s and the early part of this century: Sharp, Blumenschein, Phillips, Berninghouse, Couse, Dunton, Higgins, Ufer and Hennings are all here in 1929.

I am enjoying the beauty, the pageantry and the social life of Taos—there are parties and dances at town hall—but as winter comes I sometimes yearn for the metropolis.

"When I hear you talking about New York," I write, "and all the people it makes me a trifle wishful to go there . . . I am really in a peaceful mood

at present and don't feel I need a whirl—I really
want to work—nevertheless the thought of evening
clothes and a party occasionally does appeal. But I
have not that frantic desire for thousands of males
that I had last winter—one at a time and hand
picked is my feeling . . . It is perfectly lovely here
now—snow on the mountains—but hot as summer
in the middle of the day . . . Did I tell you that
Ernie (that's the general) is writing a book about
his experiences—it's frightfully thrilling and he's
doing it very well. I hope he can get it published
this winter."

But as the date for my departure draws near I
cannot bear to leave. Mabel encourages me to stay
on and several times I change my ticket. Then Tony
finds a little house for sale next to one of the fields
he cultivates (the Indian land is communally
owned) with a clear view across fields and pastures
to Taos Mountain. I write to Father: "Listen to this,

> 2 acres of land planted in alfalfa.
> A four room house in good repair.
> An orchard.
> A corral for horses.
> And a brook.
> In a good location off the road.
> Price $1000.

What do you think of it? . . . I am sitting up on
the roof as I write this. The sun is setting. The
mountains are very blue and peaceful and against
them is a line of marvelous golden trees."

Mabel writes Mother urging her to buy the
house. "You have no idea how much Miriam has
changed . . . She is very energetic and never lies

around lackadaisically any more. Her eyes are a deeper blue . . . She laughs and giggles all the time. She has that young Brig-general O'Malley to think of tho' she doesn't see him much for half the time she is mad at him for something and not speaking to him—but that amuses her just as much as seeing him so it's useful . . . Then Miriam is growing very thoughtful and attentive to us old ladies. Every night she takes Ella Young home to the St. Theresa house where she sleeps—makes a fire for her—and sort of fixes her up before she comes home to bed herself. She jumps up to light people's cigarettes and is thoughtful and useful in many little ways. She isn't a bit of a drag as I thought she might be if her physical condition continued to make her feel discontented and unsatisfied. She's a real asset.

"She works almost every day almost half a day and has done some good things. I think and so do others that she has a real talent only she puts it second to beaus naturally. She says nothing makes her feel so contented as having worked though. Marin said admiringly 'No one around Taos has a color sense like that little girl.'

"Now Neith, I think Miriam is one of those who have a real affinity for this country . . . for some people the vibrations are just right so that they tune into it and are able to draw life from it . . . I had that feeling the moment I arrived here first— recognized it and was happier and more myself than anywhere ever before . . . She said the other day that she didn't know before she came here there were places where people could be so happy just being alive . . . take my advice, both of you and gamble this $1,000 for Miriam who really hasn't been a happy type of child as she is now."

Mother replies: "Your letter makes me so happy about Miriam—it is like a miracle! The last two years it has been as though she had lost her real character and personality. What you describe is the real Miriam come back again—oh I am so happy and so grateful to you and so will Hutch be . . . I think he will buy that place as soon as he can. We had so much in stocks which have dropped way down but they are good and will come back but right now we are feeling rather poor . . . Very interesting about your memoirs only it's too bad we all have to be dead before they get published!"

In October Father is worried about the stock market. He is going to France and considers selling out. But two brokers, one in New York, one in Boston, advise him "don't sell." Soon after his departure the market crashes, prelude to the Great Depression. With most of his capital invested in stocks, he is far poorer than he was. He has depended on the rising market for extra income to enable him to pay for college, trips and luxuries. For a long time he expects the market to recover. Instead the depression deepens. Millions suffer poverty, hunger and despair. From now on my parents will have little to spend except for necessities. But they do not foresee that future and Father buys the house. For the next thirteen years it will be my home and the place I still love best.

I leave Taos in November, spend the holidays with Mother, Charles and Beatrix in Provincetown, then move into an apartment in Greenwich Village owned by old friends of my parents, the Torrences, who live upstairs. Olivia and Mother have been friends since before they were married, since they were reporters for New York newspapers, Mother for the *Commercial Advertiser* under Lincoln Steffens, then city editor. It was there she met my father, also a reporter. Ridgely is a poet. The apartment is unfurnished except for a bed. I buy a card table, one folding chair, glazed chintz for curtains and a few cooking pots (all will be shipped to Taos later on.) Soft coal is burned in that part of the city and cinders drift in and crunch underfoot on the bare floor. The room is large and handsome, but the emptiness and the constant battle with dirt are depressing. My knowledge of cooking is rudimentary, my attempts at entertaining, a failure. With my good friends who live on Bank Street, George and Marjorie White, I often go for a drink to Leo's speakeasy; I attend the theater, see *Show Boat* and *Green Pastures*, go out with a few young men, but I am not leading the glamorous life I envisioned. Neither am I studying, nor working at my painting, nor doing anything constructive. I make some attempts at illustration but that is not my forte. Edward comes to town and at age twenty-three I lose my virginity to him, creating a bond that is not easy for me to sever.

In early summer I return to Taos to stay with Mabel and fix up the house. Charles is to join me later. Although the house has been lived in by an elderly couple in the style in which most people in that part of New Mexico live at the time, much needs to be done to bring it up to even the simplest of our living standards. It has dirt floors, one small window in each room, no electricity, no plumbing, no fireplaces, no heating. (Whatever stoves the former tenants had went with them.) It is simply thick adobe walls, beamed ceilings with boards laid across them to support a mud roof two or three feet thick, and a falling down privy. But the surroundings make it special.

"I am working like a dog interviewing all sorts of carpenters, builders, etc." I write to my parents. "All day today I have been tête-à-têting with a salesman from the Santa Fe Builders Co. (the cheapest place to get things around here) and have finally ordered lumber for floors, window frames, window sashes, screens, locks for the doors (the locks that are on now can be opened by any key in the world), nails, hinges, molding, etc. This comes to a little over a hundred dollars including the shipping from Santa Fe. I have engaged a carpenter for $5 a day—the cheapest I can get. I can't tell exactly how long it will take him to make the frames, put in the windows, lay the floors and make the beds and bookcase—but I would imagine probably two weeks, which would be $60. The two fireplaces and whitewashing the walls will probably be about $25. Mabel is giving me an ice-box . . . I can have the house wired and electric lights put in for $30. It would be a good plan to do it, as it is safer and would probably be cheaper in the long run. Also it will be easier to put it in now before the floors are down . . . I didn't realize what a job building is. I am slowly going cuckoo. But Taos as usual is grand." Even with a second carpenter we later hired, it takes much longer than two weeks. The final cost is about $700. Neither Charles nor I have had any experience with building. We are bound to make mistakes and we do. We underestimate the time needed to complete the job; the carpenters loaf and waste material. But by the end of summer they have finished the floors and windows, put a wood-and-tar-paper roof over the insulating mud, built a little well-house and a privy. In the privy—a two-holer—they use for the seat prime two-inch-thick pine—sacrilegious waste of a noble tree. Indian women build fireplaces in three rooms (our only heat), the one in the living room designed by Tony. They replaster the walls and wash them with *tierra blanca.* I have curtains at the windows, covers on two mattresses with box springs, the card table and folding chair arrive from New York. Mabel gives me a few Navajo rugs and some dishes. We find a ram's skull with curving horns and hang it over the front door. On one side there is a view of Taos Mountain across the Indian fields and pastures, on another the apple orchard where fruit is now ripening; beyond the orchard and alfalfa field the pueblo river bounds the property. Here young Indian boys catch trout with horse-hair nooses and here Brett often fishes. On another side is the small hamlet of Placita, about a mile from Taos plaza, and the houses of our neighbors, the Martínezes and Trujillos and Spud Johnson. On the road at the end of our lane is a beautifully proportioned small adobe chapel with white wooden belfry.

My neighbors, except for Spud, are native "Mexicans" who are poor and live without electricity or plumbing. So does Spud, who when we install a bathroom about two years later, takes baths at our house. Spud's house is primitive, but cosy; in one small room are his bed, fireplace and many books;

in another his hand-operated printing press and fonts of type where he prints his *Laughing Horse* and its successor, the *Horse Fly*. The so-called Mexicans are descendants of the people who lived here when Mexico was considerably larger and a Spanish possession; their native tongue is still Spanish. Some are descendants of prosperous landowners, some merchants or professionals, but many are poor, especially in the outlying villages. Some are dry farmers—that is, they cultivate land where there is no irrigation, where the crop is principally beans. Some are sheep herders, spending their summers in the mountains, their flock and their dog their only companions. To watch the intelligent dog keeping the sheep together and in order is an experience! There is a honeyman, who observes the direction of a wild bee's flight as it leaves after drinking from a stream and tracks it to its hive in a hollow tree.

Our neighbors have small plots of land, raise a few vegetables and chickens and work as laborers wherever they can. Yet with little: sun-baked bricks of mud and straw, timbers and saplings transported by burro from the mountains, wool from their sheep, discarded tin cans—despite illiteracy, prejudice and neglect—they have created a culture, and much that is charming. The simple low lines and elongated proportions of their dwellings blend with the desert landscape; their churches are imaginative, often impressively beautiful. Santos, carved or painted in bright colors, lace and embroidery adorn the interiors. Their houses are brightened by geraniums potted in cans and set in a sunny window, by hand-loomed carpets and coverlets and homemade tin frames around pictures of saints. And their graveyards! Wooden crosses of remarkable variety of design decorated with paper flowers create sometimes a sprightly effect; sometimes in their simplicity they strike a note of stark tragedy as in Georgia O'Keeffe's *Black Cross Against Stars and Blue*, of 1929, a plain cross against Taos Mountain and the night sky. Years later, Mabel will be buried in Kit Carson cemetery. A letter from Brett in 1962 says, "Don't grieve for Mabel. She was happy to go. Her funeral was quite lovely and Mabellish. I made a painting of it, it was so lovely . . . a whole pattern has gone with Mabel."

In the year 1930, as the depression is worsening, so is the poverty of the native people. The going wage for laborers is a dollar a day; for live-in maids four dollars per week. The diet is mainly chile and beans. The prices we pay for labor and materials for the house now seem absurdly low, but it was a different world, before the war, before the consumer revolution.

There has been no formal engagement, but somehow it has become accepted by my parents and Edward's, and even by me, that I am to marry Edward. My father has called on Edward's parents and likes them both very much. "They are cultivated and civilized with evidently high character and good taste." He thinks there has been too much hesitation and that if we are sure we want to marry, we should not put it off any longer. He is worried about the material well-being of his children and perhaps he has been reassured to hear that Edward will have an income of $2,000 a year, enough at the

time to live in simple comfort. But I am still hesi-
tant. When I receive an engagement present from
Edward's mother, a beautiful negligee, bringing a
rather vague prospect close, my heart sinks. I am
not at all prepared to face the reality. My life in
Taos seems perfect as it is and I am not in a hurry
to change. Mabel, in whom I confide all my doubts,
keeps my parents informed of her analyses:

Miriam "has a terribly strong conflict over Edward going on in her. She feels it is a 'fatal' attachment between them—that she has fallen for the
wrong man. She doesn't want him to come out
here and 'spoil' Taos; neither does she want to go
East and have to marry him . . . She longs to fall
in love with someone else. But I believe she has a
kind of affinity for E . . . but that something in her
fights this and wants to thrust him away. Is this her
attachment to Hutch? Is he standing between her
and any man, unconsciously, of course? Something
in her would fight off any man (including her father) if he came too close. . . . Though she longs
for the sensuous pleasure a man gives her she is irritated with it as soon as she gets it. This seems a
good deal like that Father complex we used to hear
about."

Mother replies: "I think there is much truth in
what you say . . . about Miriam, we feel a strong
impulse to do something but realize we might do
wrong. I can't understand all that hesitation! They
ought to get married at once or quit, is my idea,
and I feel like dragging them to the altar! . .
They're two of a kind, that's the trouble—so many
strings to them they don't know which way to
go . . . I am not going to have Miriam torn up

emotionally any longer, if it has to be a shotgun wedding!"

"Well, Edward has arrived and Tony and I like him," Mabel writes in mid-September. "He is dependable—a real man and has a lot of tenderness concealed in him. He sank into the new little house and immediately cleaned up the garden and acts as though he'd always been there. Seems to suit him. He may not set the world on fire but he's a good guy and well bred—which means a lot."

I am not aware of the back and forth about me, but can feel the pressure building up from all sides. Finally I agree to be married in Taos by Circuit Court Judge Henry Kiker, who resembles Lincoln, is known as "Honest Abe" and whom I like and admire. He brings an assortment of wedding rings from Raton. Edward has brought me a beautiful watch. Once again, in a panic, I draw back, try to postpone the marriage, but now I can no longer stand against the prevailing disapproval. Edward threatens to leave and never see me again. Judge Kiker tells me he will not perform the ceremony if I put it off. Mabel is angry. I tell myself we are not committed for life, that most of my parents' friends have been divorced. At last, in a dress made of a nineteenth-century *mille-fleur* print we had brought home from Provence; with Mabel and Tony, and my parents' close friends John and Lucy Collier present, I am married to Edward by Judge Kiker, September 29, 1930. The marriage certificate is engraved with a picture of a small ship sailing a stormy, rock-filled sea.

Father writes me a sweet letter: "Dearest, dearest Miriam: Your telegram announcing the wedding has just come. Mother wept and there was a catch in my throat. That we were not with you seems hard to us, but reason says it was best so. I feel nearer to you than ever—closer in every way—more than ever your father and devoted admirer—more than ever your well-wisher. You and Trix have been the means of my real understanding of women—of the deepest sympathy I am capable of. Bless you, my darling."

Mother writes, "You and Edward must have had a nervous time those few days before your wedding! But I believe you made the right decision and cut the Gordian knot—no more doubt or hesitation! Those things eat up one's life. I remember Hemingway's remark: 'Miriam's friends must help her to get what she wants.' . . . so if any of us, or Mabel, or Judge Kiker, influenced your final decision and action, I believe we did well!" In 1923, shortly before I was to enter a Swiss boarding school, we had met the young Hemingway, then reporting a peace conference in Lausanne. I was just sixteen. He took a liking to me, walked me to the school on the night I entered, and evidently had a protective feeling, for he wrote: "It looked a fine gloomy place that night . . . I was trying to work out a powerful piece . . . It couldn't be done. Then I thought of you going into this darned big, castle like school with the long drive and the hedge and the moon and the door opening and shutting in that heavy gloomy manner and you not knowing anybody and thought you were the only brave one in the bunch . . . remember that the three of us [Lincoln Steffens and Guy Hickok, also there for the conference. My family had left for Italy.] are only a couple of blocks away and thinking about you and wishing you luck and so you're not really alone in Lausanne at all. Of course if you want to luxuriate in the feeling of being all alone and nobody within miles that's all right too."

It is exciting to be a bride. Telegrams, letters and presents pour in. Arranging the new house, laying out a garden, experimenting with cooking, being a Mrs. with a new name, doing things together—it is all fun. It is only when, a month later, we are off by ourselves, side-by-side, day after day in a Ford Roadster, travelling to Monterrey in Mexico, then through the South and finally to Boston where Edward's father is dangerously ill, that our differences begin to cause trouble. Neither Edward nor I are prepared for marriage. The old patterns of husbandly dominion and wifely submission are no longer compelling. Traditional guides are lacking; we must fumble for an accommodation of opposites.

The new road from the border to Mexico City has been finished, we are told. In El Paso I spend some of Father's generous trousseau money on lace-trimmed silk pajamas and negligee, far the largest sum I have ever had to spend as I like. We cross into Juárez, filled with bars and Americans from "dry" country, then proceed along the border to Laredo. Texas is not the "Wild West" cowboy country I expect. A chain of stores called "Helpy-Selfy" is one blow to that romantic image. Our Mexican adventure is cut short at the handsome town of Monterrey, where we learn that the road after all is far from complete; Mexican roads are even more primitive than the mountain roads of

New Mexico and information is hard to obtain. We turn back, cross endless Texas to New Orleans, then through the South and on to Boston. Very little of that trip leaves an impression: food, not usually my chief concern, assumes great importance: we lunch in diners through the West where a meal of steak, potatoes, vegetable and coffee costs 25 cents; in New Orleans there is good French cooking and old houses with lacy iron balconies; greasy meat and overcooked vegetables are the rule throughout the southern states. We quarrel, mostly about where to put up for the night. On one occasion I threaten to jump out of the car, Edward threatens to leave me behind. Rarely does he assert himself; when at home he clamps his jaws, stalks out of the room or the house; but now he and I are unable to walk away.

It is a joyous arrival on home ground. The two families have been vying for our presence at Christmas. The Brights give way and we spend the holidays in Provincetown where are many friends and parties. The atmosphere is warm, affectionate, gay. People who might in better times have been in the city or in Europe have stayed on or moved here, for Provincetown is cheap. One can almost always get free fish by going down to the dock when the boats come in. When that fails some of our artist friends eat Calo cat food sandwiches. But adversity has drawn people closer; there is that spirit of mutuality and gaiety that is often seen in the face of catastrophe, and a bottle of potent bootleg can always be had for parties.

The senior Brights have moved to Boston to be near a hospital, for Mr. Bright is ill with throat cancer. Edward and I rent a cheap apartment on Beacon Hill. Much of the time he is in Sandwich looking after his parents' house and winding up his business, while I go to work in the Theater Shop, run by an old friend, Sally Johnstone. My official title is "stylist" but I do everything from telling people they have beautiful shoulders and should wear 1850 to sewing, washing, pressing, answering the telephone—all for ten dollars a week. It is my first job and "I feel I have gone up in the world and am very self-important," I write to Mother. I learn that wealthy Boston conceals its wealth; often those who order the most expensive costumes look, in their everyday dress, seedy and down-at-heel. No conspicuous consumption here. This not just a reaction to the depression but is the old New England way of save and make-do.

Edward's parents have a Scottie, Angus, a sturdy, masterful little character, the hero of a children's book, "Angus and the Ducks." The black, shaggy little dog and I trot happily around old, rather shabby, Boston. Dogs have always been an important part of my life. So, in fact, have animals in general, tame or wild. Living in a world we cannot enter—the mysterious natural world from which our civilization more and more removes us—they connect us to a forgotten past. Dogs seem to link the two worlds; they, more than any other animal, can understand and communicate with us. And they have, inherited from their ancestor, the wolf, some of the qualities we most admire: devotion, loyalty, courage, openness.

I like Edward's parents, especially his father, who has been a factor in my attraction to his son. He is witty, charming and cultivated, a New Yorker who is more broadly sophisticated than his wife. She is the daughter of a banker from a small city in upstate New York and has inherited money. Edward Bright senior, upon the death of his father, became the owner and editor of the *Baptist Examiner*, a successful New York newspaper with a large circulation. But interest in the paper was already waning when the son took over and, after a few years, the paper failed. The family then moved to Gottingen, Germany, a university town where Edward's father became what the Germans call an *"ewige Student,"* an eternal student. There they stayed until the sudden outbreak of war in 1914. Edward attended German schools, learned to work in wood from an old carpenter, liked to work with his hands, and wanted to go on to architectural school. But his mother, adopting the German attitude that architecture was a trade, ruled it out as déclassé. This circumstance, the outbreak of war when he was eighteen, and his enlistment in the Lafayette Escadrille soon after return to the U.S., left him unprepared for any profession.

While Edward, his brother, Bobby, seven years younger, and their mother were able to return to the U.S. in 1914, Mr. Bright was mistakenly interned as a British subject. According to his son's account, he enjoyed his captivity in comfortable quarters, undisturbed by family or social demands, where he could study to his heart's content. Some months later, his wife having managed his release, he reluctantly returned to his native land and the small, isolated, town of Sandwich on Cape Cod, where Mrs. B had bought a house. There her husband found little intellectual stimulus but was sheltered from the temptation of drink. His death that first winter of my marriage is a shock and a sorrow. Not since my brother's shattered our family when I was ten has death come so near.

In early summer we attend the wedding of Edward's brother, Bobby, who has a job in New York as advertising manager of Revillon Frères, a fur house, and Katherine, a divorcee with a young son. This marriage is a hard thing for Mrs. Bright to swallow, for she holds strongly throughout her life to the belief that divorce and remarriage are morally and socially unacceptable.

Immediately after the wedding, Edward and I, Bobby and Katherine, with our Ford, embark on a coastwise steamer. We are bound for Taos via Galveston, Texas. At the end of three days crossing the seemingly endless, hot, arid plains of Texas, two in the rumble seat exposed to the southern sun, suitcases, boxes of tools, blankets, coats, golf clubs tied to the running boards, fenders and bumpers of the little car, we reach Las Vegas, New Mexico, a normal day's drive from Taos. But trouble awaits. As our overburdened car struggles up a long, steep hill beyond Mora, rain turns the adobe road into sticky, slippery mud. Even with chains we can make no progress and in turning to go back slide into a tree. Finally, having discovered the saw in a buried tool box, soaked, mud-spattered, we return to Mora. In a letter to my parents I describe our adventure: "Mora is a tiny village but very pretty. There is a lovely, old-fashioned hotel run by a friend of Billy-the-Kid. We all slept in the same room! A huge room with two double beds! And while Katherine and I went straight to bed with our bottle of whiskey (we both had cramps) the boys listened to stirring tales of frontier days from the one-eyed landlord.

"The next morning we started off gay and cheery, the sun shining and Taos only 40 miles away. We climbed the mountain (even though the mud had dried, we had to get out and walk part of the way). When we reached the summit we found woodmen at work removing a huge tree felled across the road. As we waited for them to clear the road, the rain began again." We slithered off down the steep hill, all four packed into the front seat . . . At last we struck good road and Taos was only 30 miles away! No one knows how it came about but we got lost! We climbed the highest mountain I have seen here and traversed such roads that 10 mph was really speeding . . . we came to a river flowing right across the road—it must have been fifty feet wide and two or three feet deep and very rapid . . . One by one off had to come the eleven suitcases, the heavy tool chests, the golf clubs, the tennis racket, etc. When they were all off Edward drove the car across, Katherine and I with great difficulty waded over and Bobby and Edward one by one carried over the suitcases, etc. We reached Taos late that afternoon, having gone 100 miles instead of 40. In spite of all the calamities we really had a good time and were very cheerful." He and Katherine are crazy about the country. They will return in a few years to settle in Talpa, a village near Taos, where Bobby will write and illustrate children's books.

We find our house in good condition except that the well has caved in. Beck and Paul Strand are in

the Pink House. Mabel and Georgia have quar-
relled; Georgia is staying at a guest ranch in Al-
calde, but comes to Taos to paint. Mabel, Spud tells
me, has been living the simple life in the little Two-
Story House, doing the cooking and churning butter, but is now off in the Navajo country with
Carlos Chávez, the Mexican composer. Frieda Lawrence returns to her mountain ranch with her Italian captain. "She is very nice and amusing and has
a terrific crush on Edward," I write mother. "They
gargle German to each other by the hour! The
latest thing she has done is to lend him some un-
published manuscripts of Lawrence. The Capitano
makes love to me although he doesn't speak a word
of English."

Edward and I paint in the mornings. In the after-
noons Edward lays adobe bricks for a bathroom
while a hired man mixes mud and straw for mortar.
He plants a vegetable garden between the orchard
and the river. I plant flowers—delphinium, oriental
poppies, iris, peonies, lupine—hollyhocks against
the south wall that attract several varieties of hum-
mingbird. With irrigation, our gardens flourish.
The title to the house includes the right, with certain obligations for keeping the ditch in order, to
use water from a small acequia running along our
boundary with the Indian land. When it is our as-
signed time to irrigate, we must be vigilant, for
sometimes a pirate up the line diverts the water. I
enjoy irrigating my garden: the feeling of the mud
squishing between my toes, the flowers visibly re-
sponding, birds coming to bathe in the shining
sheet under the apple trees, where we have planted
grass.

We and our friends improvise our own amusements. We hold our first annual track meet in our side field, known for the occasion as "Bright Bowl." We climb a small greased pole. I have failed in attempts to climb it before the meet, but in the excitement of the actual event, I nearly reach the top, then win the hurdles. We race, jump, do gymnastics and play ball. The neighborhood children take part. We acquire a lovable, ungainly St. Bernard puppy with enormous feet. An Indian boy brings a fledgling magpie to our door. All summer the handsome black and white bird entertains us, sleeping indoors in a cage, in the daytime scouting the neighborhood, attracted by activity, especially by anyone sawing wood. We call him Jimmy Walker after the elegant playboy mayor of New York. In the fall he vanishes. We never learn his fate but hope he has joined a flock headed south.

We go to the corn dances at Taos Pueblo and other pueblos in the area, including the big dance in Santo Domingo where five hundred Indians take part and which attracts hundreds of tourists. The costumes are beautiful. Barefoot women wear dresses of black hand-woven material off one shoulder, a bright, woven sash, bracelets and necklaces of turquoise and silver. Crowning their shining hair are light green painted shapes cut out of wood, representing trees or mountains and decorated with spruce buds. The men, bare to the waist and painted, wear thigh-length embroidered cloths and carry gourds which rattle as they dance. "There is a marvelous order in the formation of the dance," I write. "There is a hypnotic quality about the whole thing—the singing, the beat of the drums and the movements of the dancers as they indicate the falling of the rain and the growing of the corn. The whole dance lasts all day and goes on before a Christian saint of plaster of paris!"

That summer there is a long dry spell followed by a deluge out of season. During the drought strange things happen. I write my brother Charles, who is always interested in unusual phenomena: "About a week ago, the Indians heard, out at the Pueblo, a snake talking! It is a sound they haven't heard for twenty years when there was another bad drought. The same day Edward and I were at dinner when we heard a queer noise out in the kitchen. It was like someone sobbing. We found a mouse sitting behind the breadbox and really crying . . . not at all the sound a mouse usually makes! Then, the other night, we saw a moon-bow. A strange ghostly rainbow made by the moon as it was rising."

The bathroom wing progresses slowly. We have to tear off the roofs of two rooms—we find the ends of the beams are rotted. No sooner are the roofs off than the rains begin. Lumber is soaked, floors warped and Edward wallows in mud. I retreat to Brett's cabin on the Lobo mountain, where Brett and I lead the idyllic life; I paint, ride and prospect for gold, bathe in the cold mountain stream above the cabin, whence water flows through a pipe into the sink. I pick strawberries as big as robin's eggs. Mariposa lilies grow under the trees, Indian paintbrush and what I call "scarlet rain" on the slopes. I visit Frieda and Angy and the Hawks, who farm just below us and from whom we get our milk. I see wild turkeys, abundant in these mountains, and find a nest under Brett's house where rodents with long, bushy tails, known as pack rats for their habit of stealing shiny objects, have hidden tubes of Brett's mysteriously missing artist's colors.

At the end of September our first wedding anniversary coincides with the fiesta of San Geronimo. Mountains and valley flaunt their brilliant yellows. The fields yield up their multicolored corn. Red chili brightens the walls of houses and pueblo. The air is bracing. Town and pueblo celebrate with music and dancing; nobody goes to bed or does any work. There is a dinner in our honor and we go as a bride and groom of the nineties to the big costume ball. I wear a bridal gown of white satin with a high neck, leg-o-mutton sleeves, a train, a bustle, all lavishly trimmed with cheap lace. I complete the costume with white gloves, a veil and a bunch of artificial flowers pinned to my wasp waist. Purchased at McCarthy's store, the dress has been on the shelf for forty years. Edward wears a black Stetson, swallowtail coat, large pistol and cartridge belt, spit curls and the late Lord Esher's long black cape. "He looked grand," I write, "especially as he had not had a haircut all summer. When I think how much better I like him than I did a year ago, I am quite pleased."

Our little orchard is a great virtue of our place. In the warm weather we play and lounge in its shade. There are parties with a keg of beer. That fall the apple harvest is bounteous. We pick, carefully examine and pack the fruit in barrels and boxes preparatory to moving them to Spud's storeroom. We have visions of cider, applejack, apple wine, apple pie. By this time the fences are all down for the winter and, alas, during our absence for a few hours, horses come to feast. Not one apple is left to us.

At last the bathroom is finished. We have managed to get a nice old look into the little wing—there is not a single straight line. Although we are broke and in debt because of the building, we have a sense of security with our comfortable house on a small piece of land. "It was certainly a day of vision and inspiration when you bought that little house," I write my father.

Throughout the years since Mabel moved to Taos, she and my parents have corresponded sporadically. Now that I am living near her and she has become my confidante she reports frequently on her impressions and judgments of my life with Edward. The friendship of both my parents with Mabel has been long and close. Despite serious quarrels—one in 1916 when Mabel's interference between Mother and Father resulted in a temporary rupture—a strong bond has held the three together. During Mabel's stormy love affair with John Reed, author of *Ten Days That Shook the World*, an account of the Russian revolution that is now a classic, Mabel confided her thoughts and feelings to Mother when she visited our house in Dobbs Ferry and in a series of remarkable letters. And Mother, reticent by nature, was probably more open with Mabel about her marriage than with any other person; there grew up a strong woman-to-woman bond. Father and Mabel share from the beginning a restless metaphysical striving after an indefinable something they called "It."

When Edward visits the Lawrence ranch to hunt and do some work on Frieda's house, during his absence I visit Mabel for a few days. Although Mabel has found, in Tony and Taos, comparative peace and tranquillity, she still cannot resist stirring people up to create a "situation." To Father she writes, "Edward has his own peculiar satisfactions that he unhesitatingly takes, such as spending weeks in Frieda's company and he knows very well that her great, coarse, rambungchuous [sic!] nature stimulates his somewhat slow flow." Mother suspects that she is making trouble between me and Edward. She comments: "What Mabel is doing to you she tried to do to me and Pa long ago . . . You cannot trust Mabel in such matters, or be led or influenced by her. She has her fine points but when she meddles in other people's affairs she's always wrong." Mabel has indeed a strong influence on me and I am, briefly, jealous, although in a letter to Mother I proclaim: "Fortunately I have not the jealous temperament. I am not worried though very much interested and amused. Frieda is so transparent and she is going to have a hard time getting E. I am keeping strictly in the background—I don't believe in competition and rows—and enjoying it." In a way I am glad when Edward is stirred from the lethargy that seems more and more to envelop him.

Christmas is a thrilling time in the valley, a time of light. All through the town the flattish roofs of houses are lined with luminarias, candles stuck in sand in the bottom of brown paper bags. The candlelight shining through the paper is warm and soft, unlike any other light. The whole town glows. At the pueblo the Indians celebrate Christmas Eve with flaming torches, many bonfires and by shooting guns into the air. The backdrop of snow-covered mountains, the drums, the chant of the singers, half seen in the flickering light, the smoky haze combine to cast a spell, joyous yet solemn under the portentous stars. On Christmas Day we watch the deer dance symbolizing an old legend of a girl who led the deer out of the mountain to her starving, snow-bound people. A single woman, her long black hair flowing over her white buckskin dress, leads the dancers—small boys in antlered skins. In this as in all their dances, the dancing feet seem to caress the earth; in summer the dancers' motions beckon the rain to fall and the corn to grow; in winter the dance seems to honor the animals the Indians hunt. Willa Cather says in *Death Comes for the Archbishop* "It was the Indian way to pass and leave no trace, like fish through water or birds through air. It was as if . . . the spirits of earth, air and water were things not to be antagonized or aroused . . . an Indian hunt was not a slaughter . . . the land and all it bore they treated with consideration, not attempting to improve it, they never desecrated it."

We study with Emil Bisttram who has come to Taos on a Guggenheim fellowship. He teaches us how to use Dynamic Symmetry, a geometric method of organizing a painting, reportedly used by Greek and Renaissance artists. "It is sweeping Taos like an epidemic," I write my father. The Bisttrams, like nearly all our friends, are impecunious; our amusements are free. We find a hut in the mountains, import a wood stove, take our lunches and ski. I have my skis and boots from my year at school in Switzerland and can do the telemark, a turn then in use. There is no tow, all of us are novices, but at eight or nine thousand feet, the sun hot on our backs, we flounder up and down hills in deep, dry snow. Our St. Bernard, Peter Wimsey, enjoys it all as much as we do.

Edward has made a beautiful dining table, the top a thick slab of the native yellow pine; I have Mother's wedding silver, a pale lavender damask tablecloth and Italian after-dinner coffee cups from Mabel; Christmas has brought us various goodies. I am beginning to have a feel for cooking, and give my first dinner party—for Spud and John Evans— caviar served in the "most exclusive" caviar puffs; a tender steak (a great rarity in Taos) served with potatoes, vegetable and real port wine jelly, salad with lemon and garlic and olive oil, roquefort cheese with "extra special" biscuits, brandy, Benson and Hedges perfumed cigarettes. "We could talk of little else for a week afterwards. Especially as we had an argument about women that lasted four hours!"

Letters from the family bring us news of their activities, of friends, of the worsening depression. He feels extremely poor, Father writes. Every mail brings news of omission of dividends, and delay of interest. "But as long as the fundamental rhythm of life keeps on with a gay undertone, life has all the color and charm that an old man wants." All their friends in Richmond, New Hampshire, and in Provincetown are poor but there are many lively social gatherings. My parents are stimulated by their poverty to write and attempt to sell their work. Father is writing a book on drink and the virtues of the old saloon. Mother, filled with creative energy, is writing "The Town in the Forest," the life story of the village of Richmond, from wilderness to wilderness, working on a book based on Hapgood family letters from every generation back to the Revolution, as well as on plays and short stories. A story about women in business, and how that affects the family, shows that emerging as a concern. But neither of my parents is successful in marketing the work. The greatest disappointment is a near success. Mother dramatizes a story by H. G. Wells, "The Sea Lady." Arthur Hopkins, a noted New York producer, is enthusiastic, Robert Edmund Jones wants to do the sets, there is even talk of getting Greta Garbo for the lead, when H. G. Wells informs them that he will not release the rights.

But though they have many trials and disappointments during these years of the depression, there are satisfactions. Mother enjoys writing. In a letter to her old friend Arthur Bentley, a philosopher and writer, she says, "We are lucky. We have a 'hobby horse' on which we can gallop or amble to our heart's content . . . while the whole scheme of things is collapsing in ruins about us." Father and Charles, who is working on his thesis, have planted a large vegetable garden, the surplus to be canned for winter use. Father is busy driving his Ford the seven miles to the market for food, laying in wood and making beer, as well as attending to pressing family problems. Mother's sister has died and my parents have agreed to take in her eighteen-year-old daughter; they must help other members of Mother's family, as well as Trix and Luke, who are having a hard time. Father must sell his remaining stocks to meet mortgage payments on a Kansas cat-

tle ranch his father has left in trust for the grandchildren.

After Christmas they move to Provincetown.
Both Mother and Father enjoy their liquor, but
Mother complains about the increasing number of
drunks. She sometimes feels, she says, like Carrie
Nation, who with her axe smashed kegs of beer and
cases of liquor in the saloons of New York. In Provincetown, with its long coastline, it is easy to come
by booze, even easier than in inland towns, though
in most of the country Prohibition has become a
farce. On gala days the beaches are littered with
cases of liquor dumped overboard by smugglers
when revenue cutters are closing in.

In the early thirties the town of Provincetown is
bankrupt, unable to pay its employees, the banks to
whom it is indebted or to fix the roads. Seventy-
five houses are for sale for taxes. In Taos the state
passes a bill to take the property of anyone who is
not fully paid up on taxes. This means just about
everyone, including us and Mabel. The whole
country is suffering. In the nation there is much labor unrest. Mother writes news of their friends:
John Dos Passos and Theodore Dreiser have been
arrested for "criminal syndicalism" in connection
with a miners' strike in Kentucky. They could go to
jail for twenty-one years. President Hoover urges
people to buy goods, especially automobiles.
Mother writes a friend, "I hope you followed dear
Herbert's advice and bought a few automobiles as a
patriotic duty . . . How to pay taxes? Just trade in
the new automobiles." In contrast, Edward's
mother, who is still much better off than my par-

ents, is violent in her denunciation of Roosevelt, to whom she attributes all her troubles.

In the villages surrounding Taos, poverty is often extreme. South of Santa Fe, in the mining town of Madrid, where the company puts on a great show of Christmas lights, the company houses behind the lights are shocking in their misery—flimsy, rickety and lacking even rudimentary comfort. Closer by I see a baby in the last stage of starvation owing to overwatered milk. Our first winter in Taos is a hard one. Old timers say it is the worst in memory— lots of snow, extreme cold, then a thaw when the mails can't get through and Taos is an ocean of mud. At its coldest, the temperature is 33 degrees below zero. There are nights when we hear horses breathing outside our window where they lean against the walls for warmth. All gates are opened in the fall, animals turned loose to exist as best they can; when snow is deep, many die; in spring their bones lie in the fields. That same winter of 1931–32 Edward and I have our own experience of the deadly cold. I write my parents about it: Edward is in hospital in Santa Fe with a deep and painful infection in his right hand requiring surgery. When I return from an overnight visit to him, although I have hired a neighbor to keep up the fires, I find everything frozen solid, the hot water heater burst, a lot of pipes burst, the pump broken. "I must get busy now and stoke my seven fires." These are fireplaces and kitchen range. By the following winter we have acquired oil heaters.

In the spring the roads are deep mud, dust blows in over the mountains from the arid plains, and the town suffers a traumatic change. "Last Sunday Rome burned!" I write. It is the first of two disastrous fires that destroy about half the buildings on the plaza. "At 2:30 Edward and I leapt out of bed at the sound of the siren and beheld the sky of Taos an angry red. I was dressed in two minutes—Edward carefully washed, dressed, tied his shoes, combed his hair and was about to shave and manicure his nails when I stopped him by main force and we rushed to the scene of action. It looked as if the whole town would go. The pool hall was gone and the Plaza Hotel in flames when we arrived—it was so hot in the plaza you couldn't stand it. Then the bakery, meat market, cafe and drug store caught and they blew up the courthouse to stop it going any further . . . the explosion broke all the windows for acres around. But it didn't help a bit and the flames leaped over the courthouse and burned Bond-McCarthy's huge store to a cinder. The bank was next and everybody thought it would go, but suddenly the wind turned and that together with the fact that McCarthy's walls were fireproof cement kept it from going any further in that direction, but it went back and burnt out a whole block of little houses behind. If the wind hadn't changed it would have burnt the whole town, literally. As it was it burnt all one side of the Plaza. It threw maybe one hundred people out of work and the town is terribly depressed. Edward spent most of his time helping move out the dentist's chair . . . and I chauffeured artists who were rescuing their pictures from the other hotel which they thought would burn. The ruins burned for three days."

In the midst of the excitement, the crowd of

onlookers, the firemen pumping from a town well, I witness a strange sight: a man with a tablespoon ladling water from a puddle into a small can, then carrying it to the fire and throwing it on the flames. Only Brett sleeps through it all.

The mud dries. Tumbleweed rolls across the desert and piles up against the fences. As warmth greens the fields, the gates are closed once more and the cattle confined. Wild plum are masses of white along the water courses. Soon our orchard is a pale pink glory. A sudden heavy fall of wet snow descends on each tree like an ermine cap, then melts away. Tony is planting field corn for his animals in the adjacent field he and his nephews are cultivating. Pueblo land is owned in common, but Tony will have the use of this field, which lies along one border of our property, for the next few years.

In July, my sister Beatrix drives out with Marjorie Content, her two children and a young archaeologist, Gordon Grant. She will spend the summer with us while Marjorie, a photographer, Gordon and Georgia O'Keeffe will tour the West in search of the remains of ancient civilizations. Later, Gordon will return and take Trix to several pueblos where he will exchange songs with the other tribes. Trix and I have a good time. On a two-night pack trip into the mountains, where the air is so thin she cannot sleep, Trix's horse decamps during the night; she must mount a large pack horse—he must be a race horse, she thinks, for he takes control and bolts down the corkscrew trail for home. We swim in the Rio Grande, a narrow, boulder-strewn river here, where hot springs bubble up in places. We go to hot springs where one bathes in a dark, covered pool in whose shadows Trix is afraid some enormous spider lurks; outside is a shallow pool where Indians wash their blankets and their long black hair. As usual, for she is beautiful, Trix has several young men hanging around. On her birthday we have a murder party (as everyone is reading and writing detective stories, all the rage at that time). Judge Kiker presides as judge, Dr. Gertrude Light is coroner, Trix Chief of C.I.D., I am attorney for the defense and likewise accomplice in the murder of Maria Magdalena.

Peter, the dog, tangles with a huge porcupine; he comes home with quills three and four inches long in his mouth, tongue and muzzle. We pull many out, but soon the pain becomes so great that he will not submit. There is no vet in Taos, but a kind doctor agrees to come. He administers chloroform while he extracts the remaining quills. But suddenly Peter is no longer breathing. The doctor gives him artificial respiration and, after a moment, we all breathe again. Jimmy the magpie hides butter in the folds of the curtains. He perches on my head and when Mabel visits, tries to perch on hers. She keeps parrots and pigeons, but has a horror of touching birds and runs screaming around the orchard, Jimmy in pursuit.

While I am enjoying many aspects of my life in Taos, it seems I am complaining to Mabel of Edward's increasing self-isolation, for she fires off another report to my parents: "It is time for Edward and Miriam to do something about their life together to save it." Mother is puzzled for Trix's and my letters mention nothing wrong. It is true that Edward is spending more and more time at the La

Fonda hotel on the plaza drinking coffee and playing chess. According to Mabel, he is also eating breakfasts and dinners there even though we are serving them at home. Mabel thinks our rather amateurish cooking may be to blame. Am I failing in my wifely duties? Trix and I get up early, cook big breakfasts, for dinner serve steak with several vegetables, but Edward still haunts the hotel. In Sandwich he had spent much time at the local inn where he also played chess; perhaps it is a habit first formed in German cafes where by custom men spent their leisure hours. It is part of an almost imperceptibly gradual process, what will be a long fading away. While I am bothered enough to complain to Mabel, my love for life in Taos, my work and my friends, the grandeur of the place overshadow the increasing distance between me and my husband.

After Trix leaves, Edward's mother comes for a visit. Inevitably, she and Mabel dislike each other. Although they both come from well-to-do families in upstate New York and both have lived many years in cosmopolitan surroundings abroad, they are at opposite poles in their views of the world. Mrs. Bright, as I always call her, tolerant in many ways, yet clings to the old taboos, all of which Mabel has flouted. She disapproves violently of Mabel and thinks her a bad influence on us; Mabel can't stand her rather conventional type and of course the gossips are busy with stories that Mrs. Bright is attempting to take over our household, to rescue her son from evil influences. Mabel says she works against me in an underhanded way. At the same time Mrs. Bright is writing my parents of Mabel's kindness to our family. With her in the house, Edward perks up, works at his painting and enjoys his mother's visit. I hear some of the gossip, but I too like having her around. She is amusing, she brings her son to life, and brings her domestic knowledge and a certain gaiety into our little household.

Mrs. Bright's disapproval may stem in part from the unflattering talk one hears in the East when Mabel's name is mentioned, that she has kidnapped Tony, is about to leave him for another man, is always making trouble, etc., etc. Or she may have read Mabel's book *Lorenzo in Taos*, published in February 1932, in which Mabel paints a quite repellent portrait of herself and her wilful intrusion into other lives. There is no doubt much truth in this picture, for Mabel does use her powerful will upon others in order to bring about what she sees as a good result, but her portrait doesn't do justice to her more attractive side—the side that drew Lawrence while he continually fought against and condemned her use of will to direct his life. She wanted him, as she said herself, to see through her eyes in writing about Taos and the Indians. While he could not do that, it was her dauntlessness, "her grim Yankee dauntlessness," that he most admired, he says in a letter. Yet it was the very quality that drove him to fury.

Many years before, Father had written her during one of their quarrels that she lacked that fundamental respect for personality, that noninvasiveness that is essential to the life of the artist. Now he writes her about *Lorenzo*, "It is quite wonderful that you were able consciously to reveal the many-sided and conflicting elements of your own character, being willing apparently to reveal the shadows with the lights. The two men, Tony and Lawrence, come out beautifully, in really brilliant portraiture. You yourself have not escaped so happily. . . . His [Lawrence's] instinct against some of your enthusiasms, such as Gurdjieff et al., struck in me a sympathetic feeling. The tendency in you, so marked, to seek restlessly an impossible significance in life, he constantly tried to modify and normalize. In that way, his effect on you might have been the same as Tony's—obviously has been, except for the fact that you expected from Lawrence something which it was impossible for him truthfully to give." Mabel describes Lawrence as demanding that other people be as simple as himself. She quotes a letter he wrote to her: "I wish to heaven you would be quiet and let the hours slip by. But you say it's not your nature. You'll say it is your nature to 'do things' to people, and have them 'do things' to you. That wearies me. Even you apply your will to your affection. . . ."

The following year Mabel publishes the first volume of her memoirs, *Background*, an account of her early life in Buffalo. Again she paints a harsh picture not only of her family but of herself. To me Father writes his opinion that while parts of it are very interesting, he thinks it not very truthful. She has made a highly selective choice. "I don't believe in the picture she made of Buffalo, striking though it is . . . it is too striking. . . . There is a morbid desire in it to exaggerate the things calculated to hit people between the eyes. But yet there are very vivid things which stick in the memory . . . Mabel's impatience makes it impossible for her to be dull. It would be a better book, however, if there were longer passages of dullness in it. It would be nearer the reality of life." Mabel herself is not satisfied with her work. "At present I am perfectly dissatisfied with all the work I have done these past 10 years—all those fat vols," she writes him. "They seem one-sided to me—too negative. The one I want to write about Taos—Tony—the Indians, I feel unequal to—not enough deep understanding." She seems unable to "avoid a slight effect of caricature of myself and companions. I think I had it all the time inside me until I came out here and became more true and real as a character . . . in my whole life before Taos and Tony, [there was] a slightly ridiculous touch and it seems to have surrounded many people and events beside myself—all except Neith who emerges seriously lovely, cool and individual."

No, Mabel is not dull. She is always stirring up something interesting, always impatient. On one occasion, deciding to get a permanent wave, which necessitates being attached to a machine, she becomes bored halfway through the process. She pulls herself loose and leaves the beauty parlor with lank, wet hair. Another time, when I am there for dinner by myself, her friends Eve and Jack Young-Hunter telephone to ask if they can bring over a visitor whose portrait Jack is painting. He owns vast farming acreage and is known as the "Montana Wheat King." Mabel agrees but when there is a knock at the door, she jumps up, runs into the Rainbow Room, with a "Miriam, you cope," and I am left to handle the embarrassed Young-Hunters. Their guest, clearly a man of wide interests and diplomacy, has just returned from a trip to Russia. I enjoy an hour of interesting talk about his experience; the Young-Hunters are grateful to me that the visit has not ended in disaster. When I look into the room where Mabel must be, for there is no exit except through the living room, she is missing. She has jumped out the window, several feet from the ground.

It is never dull at Mabel's. Something is always going on. "Never a dull moment" is one of her favored expressions at moments when things are happening too fast. She makes them happen, always thinking up things to do: a girl from the beauty parlor to give us all facials, Brett to paint the windows and the lampshades, Manuel to carve the doors, Ralph to haul large flat stones from the river to pave the big courtyard where she will scatter seeds to root in the crevices and become a forest of red white and pink hollyhocks where hummingbirds sup. There are parties, often with Indian dancers, Trinidad and his group, who perform the spectacular eagle dance among other secular dances. She introduces me to many experiences of the country, the pueblo and to people I would not otherwise have known. Her gossip and her comments are fun. Life in Taos would not have been as glamorous without her. She is the center of a way and style of life; it is the same thing she did in her New York salon days; she has created an atmosphere which draws people and to which they in turn contribute. Carl Van Vechten, an old friend, said of her: "It is that vital, buoyant spirit in you that we love! The creative, forward-looking spirit."

Through her friendship with my parents, I have been acquainted with Mabel since I was a child. It was probably at Mabel's suggestion that, when I was about seven, I spent a few months at the Duncan School in Croton-on-Hudson, where Mabel had a house, during my sister's illness with t.b. of the glands. Elizabeth Duncan, sister of the dancer, Isadora, had moved her school from Germany upon the outbreak of war. Mabel's son, John, was also a pupil there, the only boy, who wore Greek-style tunics like the rest of us, dark blue every day, sky blue for best. In the spring we trooped into the fields, filled our arms with wild flowers and that night cast them in the path of Isadora as she danced in Madison Square Garden.

I remember Mabel from Provincetown days, when she was there with Maurice Sterne living in the abandoned life-saving station by the ocean at Peaked Hill, later the summer home for a few years of Eugene O'Neill and his family. It was Mabel who turned the place into a home with her remarkable ability to create an environment. Even as a child I was struck by the beauty of the old building. The lines were long, low and expansive like the facing sea. As one entered the large living room where life-boats had once been kept, it seemed cool and calm. The colors of walls, floor and old braided rugs were white, gray and sea-blue. It was sparsely and comfortably furnished with chairs upholstered in those colors and antique Colonial furniture probably puchased at the John Francis general store where in those days we got all the necessities. Two gray Persian cats asleep in the chairs added to the sense of peace. I visited her a few times in Croton when I was at college. But until Taos, she was simply a friend of my parents, I had little impression of her personality.

In Taos she becomes a kind friend, a companion, a confidante, in a way, a mother figure. Perhaps she regards me as her child. She looks out for me, gives me many presents, takes me along on trips, includes me in her small circle of habitués, takes a personal interest in my life. Although Mabel quarrels at one time or another with most of her friends, we never quarrel. There is no occasion. Her good opinion means too much to me to risk provoking her or to question her actions. I like her, enjoy her, respect and am fond of her, and am grateful for the part she has played in bringing me out of the doldrums. She has given me a secure place and reassurance when I needed it. At first I am unsure, uncomfortable with my contemporaries in Taos, who seem very sophisticated, who dress in faded blue jeans, concho belts, big hats and cowboy boots, while I have only riding breeches, Eastern-style city boots or cotton dresses. With Mabel and her circle I feel at home.

I see how she often hurts other people, but I also see how generous she is, not only to me but to struggling artists, to others in need, to the town and the pueblo. To the town she gives a bandstand in the plaza and, for a hospital, a beautiful house she has built. Her charities are done quietly, unknown even to her close friends. There is the usual jealousy and widespread criticism of Mabel. I often feel called upon to be her defender.

Our relations are on a different level from hers with my parents, with Frieda and D. H. Lawrence or Robinson and Una Jeffers, friends with whom she shares her inner life. She likes companionship; I am young, eager for experience, responsive, in love with life in Taos. Tony is often away during the day and a good many evenings. He has his own interests, his farming, his Indian and Mexican dances and parties, his many nephews. I sometimes wonder about their relationship, how they bridge the huge gap between their cultures and experience. Tony cannot read or write. The Taos Indians have no written language; he grew up before the Indian Service schools taught children English. The whole world of books and Western ideas is closed to him. In my presence their talk is of practical things or of people. Mabel relies on Tony's judgment of people. He has taught her about farming and the life of the pueblo and the valley about which she writes so movingly in *Winter in Taos*. But much of Tony's life is closed to her as hers is to him—the life of the kiva, the underground chamber where the men go before their ceremonial dances, the ceremonies at Blue Lake—all these are secret, never to be revealed. In a poem printed in *Lorenzo in Taos* Mabel writes: "Ah you! you alien! you perpetual stranger for whom/I so completely give up all else!/ . . . are you leagues away?/Are you off in the night, winding a silent trail/Up the mountain to the never-forsaken shrine?/Are you hidden with your brother in some dark cave,/Sitting before a cedar fire in the secret, forbidden peyote rites?/Ah, lost! lost to me in other worlds, wrought by the subtle peyote dreams!/Most incomprehensible for the white woman/Who crosses over into the Indian heart!"

Although I do not realize it fully at the time, there is no doubt something very wrong with Edward. He does not talk to me about it but has told others he feels unused, bored, isn't getting anywhere. He is depressed, lacks initiative. I encourage him in his painting, for I have real faith, as do others, in his original gift, but he does not apply himself. I do not understand what is wrong or how to deal with it. I enjoy the place and my life there in spite of the cloud enveloping my husband. Most of my letters home at this time convey high spirits. Perhaps Edward resents my enjoyment of life, my friends, the strong influence of Mabel, but he never talks about it, simply goes along while isolating himself. Mabel likes Edward and frequently has us to dinner. When we leave the table he goes into the Rainbow Room where he stays alone playing records. Mabel tells Father, "Poor Edward has no deep interests except war and chess, apparently." I confide to Mabel that in the last few months things have gotten worse. But there are brief bursts when he comes to life: on our trip to Mexico, when he studies with Maurice Sterne; after our two children are born. But he soon disconnects. Am I his tenuous hold on life? Is that why he has persisted five years in his pursuit?

While Mrs. Bright stays on with Edward, I go east for Christmas with my parents. I am to meet Edward later in Mexico. The family are gathered on the farm in Richmond. We burn whole trees in the big fireplace, sit down to a bountiful table, the vegetables, beer and cider, home-made or grown. The atmosphere is warm and gay. It is cold going to the woodpile and the outhouse; the car is hard to start, the ruts frozen in the dirt roads. As mother says, "a

few queer birds are frozen in with us": a refugee
Colonel of Cossacks who does Russian dances, a
Scotsman, who sometimes wears his kilts; both are
close to destitute. The colonel has built himself a
small cabin in the woods; he works on the roads to
pay his taxes; on his primitive table is a picture of
the czar and his family in a silver frame.

Soon after the first of the year, I take a boat from
New York to Veracruz. From there I go by train to
Mexico City, where I am to meet Edward. He and
Dr. Gertrude Light, a physician now living in
Ranchos de Taos, but formerly practicing in New
York, among the first women to do so, and Edward
(the Bright-Light expedition) have driven from Taos
over the now completed (after a fashion) road from
the border. I am very glad to see my husband and
our stay of several months in Mexico seems like a
honeymoon. We stop a few days in Cuernavaca, a
beautiful small city of old houses, tropical trees and
murals by Diego Rivera. His work impresses me,
and the paintings I do in Mexico are heavily influenced by his style. We have rented John Evans's
house in Taxco—$25 a month including a cook, a
man to look after the garden, a horse, four parrots,
two ducks, a rooster. The cook does the marketing
and our food costs us sixty cents a day. Taxco is a
picturesque town; steep hills surround a small plaza
with its large, ornate church. Our small house of
pinkish stucco with a tiled roof is perched high up
one of the hills overlooking the plaza. On the frequent feast days, fireworks are set off from the roof
of the church and sometimes land on our portal.
The sound of exploding rockets, singing, bells ring-
ing, donkeys, much used for transporting produce

and other goods, braying in the ravines, dogs bark-
ing, cocks crowing, all float up to us. Once I awake
in the night to a man's song of love, a pure voice
capturing for me the romance of that place.

There are few Americans. The Mexican revolution is only a few years in the past and I feel hos-
tility from some of the young. Americans are
intruders and all appear rich. Unquestionably poverty is widespread, but not obvious. There are few
beggars. In that warm climate there is not the kind
of misery we are seeing in the United States. The
dogs are skin and bone, scavengers who roam the
barrancas where they find a few scraps of unwanted
food. One night I hear a crunching sound on our
path; there is a dog eating a few spilled kernels of
dried corn. We like and see a good deal of John Her-
man and his wife, Josephine Herbst, both journalists. With them Edward unbends and takes part in
the gaiety. Marsden Hartley, a painter and friend of
my parents and later to become one of Edward's
few friends in New York, stays a few days on his
way from the coast where he has contracted the
"turista." We hire a little boy to pose for us, then a
young woman. We wander down to the plaza and
sometimes visit the surrounding villages. Once we
attend a play—like the medieval miracle plays I
have read about, with its three-tiered stage, the
people below, the nobility and clergy on the middle
stage and royalty above. At the end, the martyred
heroine is hoisted in a basket from the stage to the
church steeple. Our stay is peaceful and unevent-
ful. "I thought I was a sociable animal," I write my
parents, "but maybe I was meant to be a hermit after all. We sit calmly on our hill, reading, painting,

studying Spanish or playing dominoes—occasionally wandering down to the plaza for a bottle of beer . . . Edward is much more sociable and full of life than he used to be when first he emerged from that dreadful Sandwich! How I loathe that place when I think of the horrible life he must have led there."

There are fleas everywhere. Scorpions by the dozens descend our walls at night. We find them in our clothes and shoes. They are ugly, menacing creatures, with a stinging tail arched over the back, but evidently are not very dangerous, for when Edward is stung, the remedy prescribed by the pharmacist (there is no doctor), ten drops of iodine in a glass of water and plenty of cognac, is efficacious. Toward the end of February we leave for Oaxaca, where we will meet Dr. Light and the Strands. We have been warned about the road but since information about Mexican roads is sketchy and often proves wrong, we decide to go ahead. But the warnings have been grossly understated. In many places the rough road becomes a track which wanders off and loses itself in dusty fields. It is hot. Our way lies mostly over flinty desert mountains where only great spectral cactus grow. One day of the three-day journey, the road, wide enough for one car, is cut into a cliff. We encounter only one vehicle, a truck going in the other direction. When we pass, our wheels are on the very edge of the precipice; I look down hundreds of feet to the rocks below. We spend a night in a hotel where we are registered as Señor and Señora Gringo. On the third day we have descended to a plain where the dust rises in clouds through the floor of the car. It seems in our ignorance we are become pioneers. The newspaper next day carries a headline "Americanos drive from Mexico City in powerful car" (our Ford). I cannot bear to think of the return journey.

A recent earthquake has wrecked many fine old houses and churches in the city center but life goes on seemingly undisturbed. With Paul and Becky Strand we visit the markets and go about the countryside and to neighboring villages where Paul photographs the churches while I draw. We marvel at the tree of Tule, thought to be 4,000 years old, its trunk nearly 200 feet in circumference, its branches spread wide enough to encompass a house. We visit the markets where villagers display their fruits, vegetables, blankets, clothing, baskets, pottery, ornaments of tin or straw, all brilliantly colored, their imaginative creations, always artistic, often beautiful. Untutored, they work in an old tradition and have an instinctive sense of rightness. Out of ordinary materials at hand these people, very poor by our standards, fashion a remarkable array of useful and charming objects: a small merry-go-round with its horses, all of straw, animals and people of straw and tin, or papier mâché, each one individual, nothing manufactured or imported. These people have an exuberant creativity and natural taste, as yet uncorrupted. We buy blankets and small objects that will not take up much room in the car.

"The people are marvelous as are all the Indians of Mexico," I write in a letter. "They are so calm and graceful and unworldly. They never hurry. They can relax as completely on a stone pavement as we can on a feather bed. The women carry great burdens on their heads and hold themselves like queens. If you buy from them it's all right but if you don't they don't really care. They are interested only in the barest necessities. They can live very comfortably on a few cents a day and don't want any more. They seem to have a marvelous time. There is always a fiesta. They celebrate everything—and their church and their religion, they make the very most of that. They use their amazing ingenuity and versatility for their own edification—not to sell. Their clothes are gay and becoming. Their dishes—even the cheapest cooking pot—are hand made and decorated with birds and flowers. Their burros have red and yellow girths and bridles and carry fruits and vegetables to market in gay baskets and pots . . . They have fine figures and are very handsome. I feel like a scrawny little white earthworm when I am among them."

On Good Friday we watch a Penitente ritual. A man descends, on his knees, from a nearby mountain, his back torn and bleeding from the thorns of an organ cactus strapped across his shoulders as in the arms of a cross. The Brotherhood believe that only by shedding one's blood can he be redeemed. In Taos there are remnants of these practices, forbidden and secret, Mabel says, in the Penitente morada a half-mile into the desert behind her house.

I am greatly relieved when Paul offers to take my place in the car for the drive back to Mexico City. Beck and I return by the little train that puffs and slithers its way around the steep grades and curves of the mountains. We stay a few weeks in the city, where Beck and I wander about to the shops which offer many goods from Europe. I buy some French lace and a papier mâché sheep's head, still hanging in my house, made by some humble artist from a musical score. Then Edward and I set out for home in our well-traveled Ford. The new road, still primitive and unfinished in places, climbs mountains, crosses burning lowlands. There the hood of the car, where the gas tank is located, is too hot to touch. It is the last long trip for our valiant little car.

When we return it is spring; we work on our house and garden. Edward makes a desk, replaces the flimsy doors with thick pine, knocks a hole in the wall and puts in French doors. Mabel gives us a homespun carpet—squares of rose and soft yellow—I paint the living room floor rose. The curtains are homespun yellow wool. A crayon drawing of mountains, a parting gift from Marin, a flower painting on glass by Becky Strand, and the portrait of an Indian boy by Brett adorn the walls. Over the years we add more rooms to form an ell embracing the orchard and the view of Taos Mountain beyond. We plaster the outer walls with *tierra bayeta* [*sic*], a cream-colored earth. Edward does much of the building. One of the new rooms, built when we are expecting our second child, has a ceiling of cedar, split, its rose heart and white outer parts exposed to form stripes and laid in a herringbone pattern. I mix *tierra blanca* and a red earth dug from the roadside on the way to Albuquerque to paint the walls. I have a pink-painted antique bedstead.

I am to exhibit two of my Mexican paintings at the Harwood Foundation and am making a little money painting trays to order. Mabel orders a large one of Tobias and the Angel—Tobias holding a fish. Leopold Stokowski, conductor of the Philadelphia Symphony, often visits Mabel. This summer he is here with his wife, Evangeline, their two daughters and two large dogs. They order a picnic scene. I manage to get them all on a large tray, including dogs, Brett, Tony and an Indian friend in a grove of trees—and "pretty good likenesses!" "Stokey," as he is called, is friendly, unpretentious and amusing. He is a fan of western movies; at the local theater we sit in loges, enormous rocking armchairs. One year "Blumy," Ernest Blumenschein, one of the early artists, is complaining loudly about the film *Gone With the Wind*, when Mrs. Bert Phillips, a very proper lady, yells across the theater, "Oh shut up old sourpuss!" Another time Stokey is here for Christmas. At our house for the lighting of the tree, we follow (for the last time) our family custom of lighted candles. Our three-year-old son, Ned, goes too close, the crotch of his red and green plaid overalls catches fire, Stokowski is the first to spring forward and puts out the flames with his hands—his indispensable white hands that Brett will paint over and over again in the act of conducting.

She has found her new hero. In the winter she will follow him to Philadelphia where she will paint innumerable portraits. "Here I am producing a winged Apollo . . . Stokowski is so busy I have to throw bombs at him to make him remember my existence and yet he has broken all his iron-clad rules for me and I have sat in the Holy of Holies and watch him at all concerts," she writes me.

A group of us celebrating San Geronimo fiesta

discover that a guest in a hotel on the plaza is a violinist in the Philadelphia Symphony Orchestra. He has not brought his instrument, but our host produces a battered violin taken in payment for a room. To what seems to me at the time the most beautiful music in the world we dance barefoot in the moonlit square.

We have been thinking of having a child. I ask my parents if they believe it is worthwhile to have children. Father replies: "You might as well ask whether it is worth while to live or not. It is one of the results of life, part and parcel of the whole shebang. I don't think a woman can develop in the way nature intended without children. She cannot arrive at her full beauty or her balanced understanding of life otherwise. Of course they are causes of the greatest pain sometimes, as well as the greatest pride and satisfaction . . . but a vital person cannot hesitate to take the chance." I too feel that I do not want to miss one of life's important experiences and so, in the late fall of 1933, I am excited to find myself pregnant. Edward seems equally pleased.

Upon receiving my letter, Father replies to my "thrilling and moving news. You have always been a very precious person to me and now you are even more so. I wish I could be with you all the time for the next few months, not that I could do much for you. I would just like to be there." Father has a good deal of the feminine in him and often says he would have liked the experience of bearing a child.

Mother's reaction is unexpected: "I am so overcome by the great news—I didn't think I would feel this way at being a grandmother, I thought I would be bored! And instead I am very happy. Ain't nature wonderful?" and then she gives me a bit of advice: "Do not allow yourself to be fussed by any visitors—and do not argue, let that go by like the idle wind that you regard not! Remember that parents when they get on in years are bound to have their little ways and that you will sometime have yours! and make allowances. I have great sympathy for parents and so will you when you are one."

We decide to have the baby in the East. In the fall we drive across the grim, drought-parched Great Plains, stopping in Chicago for the World's Fair, then on to visit our families. For the winter months we share a house with Bobby and Katherine Bright, their baby daughter and Katherine's young son. She is pregnant with their second child, due at about the same time as mine. The house in South Norwalk on a point of land jutting into the Sound, gated enclave of the rich, we rent for fifty dollars a month. For another fifty dollars we hire a cook and her son, who is handyman during the day, then puts on a white coat to serve dinner. Bobby's salary is fifty dollars a week; with Edward's small income we live in luxury that winter of the deep depression. The two brothers commute to New York, Edward to study with the artist Maurice Sterne. I keep busy painting and selling my trays. For all of us it is a happy winter. After the first three months of pregnancy I feel well and energetic, Maurice is encouraging and we all look forward to the birth of our children. I do not often see the misery on the streets of New York.

My doctor in the city is a warm and caring man, Harry Lorber, who has looked after our family and

many of our friends for years. His office on lower
Park Avenue is a small museum, the paintings of
many of his patients, including Georgia O'Keeffe,
on the walls. In glass cabinets are his collection of
ancient Chinese artifacts and covering his desk photographs of the many babies he has delivered.

In the spring the owners of the house return and
we exchange our posh life-style for a simple cottage
in the woods of Westport. Edward is still studying
with Maurice, I am filling orders for trays and enjoying this period of quiet. I contemplate the spring
woods through the open door of the privy. The
only excitement is my sister's sudden marriage.
She has been working in the city for a theatrical
and literary agency where she has met and without
notice to anyone has married a young writer, Luke
Faust. Our parents are distressed at this hasty marriage to a man they know nothing about and are
saddened that they have been absent during the
marriage of both their daughters. Although Mother
is not generally interested in the conventions, I
think she looked forward to staging a wedding in
her garden at Richmond. She herself had been
given a church wedding, with all the trappings.

After the newly-weds visit us, I write a reassur-
ing letter: "Trixie glows and beams . . . the hard-
boiled, cynical look has vanished . . . Father would
be amused to hear that her one ruling idea now is
the quiet, regular life. If she wouldn't take care of
herself, she is going to take care of Luke! She was
laying into him for eating too fast, smoking too
much and she continually quotes you, Father, on
the subject of health, food and conduct!"

My parents have been spending the winter in

Provincetown. In her constant need to create, Mother has in the past few years in addition to writing taken up rug-hooking. Now she is making one for me from my design of a turquoise horse. She is trying to get a dress that is just the right color for the horse from Mary Vorse. "She promised it to me year before last when it got too short for her. . . . It is now about up to her knees but the miserable creature says she has discovered she can wear it as a smock . . . but you ought to see her!" Mary Heaton Vorse is a friend from early days in New York, a member, with my parents, of the group that launched the Provincetown Players in 1915. She is a writer best known for her coverage of the labor movement.

Early in June we move into the city to stay at the Hotel Brevoort where Mother and Father will join us for the great event. Three weeks go by beyond the expected date. I am uncomfortable, it is hot, I try to move things along by riding Fifth Avenue buses, climbing the swaying stairs to the seats on top. Worried, the doctor twice gives me castor oil. Even that does not work. Finally, in the hospital, he administers a powerful drug to bring on labor and Ned is born, long, thin and blue, but healthy. I see him only at nursing time. I have never before seen a new-born; I have never held a baby. In this era of the depression, babies are scarce among the people I know. I enjoy my stay in the hospital, the first days of motherhood, but when at the end of six days I am discharged, I am at sea. How will I take care of this fragile creature? What if I drop him? What about that soft spot on his head? Will he suffocate in the middle of the night? We hire a nurse for two

weeks, for the trip via boat and train to Cape Cod.
For all of us it is an adventure: she has never been
out of New York City, I must suddenly learn to be a
mother, Edward a father.

I follow to the letter the federal government's
book on baby care: regular hours of nursing, sleeping, cuddling, playing; at a specified age orange
juice (the orange cut with a sterilized knife), freshly
prepared beef juice (there are no prepared foods for
babies except Pablum), cod liver oil. Everything is
sterilized, diapers boiled; if I have any sign of a cold
I wear a gauze mask. Don't pick up the baby every
time he cries, keep away from crowds, noise and
germs. Mrs. Bright, with whom we spend a week
in Sandwich before settling for the summer in
Provincetown, is spoiling him, I think; she can't
bear to hear him cry. After the nurse leaves I
scarcely sleep what with nursing every three hours,
changing, bathing, listening at night for the baby's
breathing. We hire a young woman at seven dollars
a week to help with the housework, but I never
leave her with Ned. I paint a few trays, but do virtually nothing for the next year but care for the
baby. We see very few people although I have
friends in Provincetown. I am a fanatical mother, so
totally preoccupied with motherhood that I can't
have been very good company. Fortunately, Edward
is painting steadily. Mrs. Bright comes to stay
while he escapes for a while to New York to resume
his sessions with Maurice.

That winter we stay with our costume designer
friend, Sally Johnstone, and her husband, Bard, in
their charming old house in Orleans. It is there that
Sally has her summer theater among the grove of

locust trees; it is there that I first met Edward. Sally has been like a second mother to me ever since the summer after my brother died, while my mother was lost to everything but her grief, and though Sally was a stranger to me, I flung myself into her arms as she walked up the path to our door. I enjoy her household. Sally makes her costumes; "Snooky," as we call him, naps on the porch; he gains weight steadily; before dinner he has his play time; in the evening Bard reads aloud from *Gil Blas*. On the radio is the gruesome story of the Lindbergh kidnapping trial. It is a pleasant interlude before we set out once more for Taos.

The family are scattered. Luke and Trix, who is pregnant, have been forced to move into Luke's parents crowded and noisy household. When the baby, Lukie, is a few months old, Luke gets a job on the *Bridgeport Times Star*. Bridgeport is booming with the growth in the munitions industry, apartments are scarce and expensive; they are having a struggle to make ends meet. Charles is teaching at a new school in Putney, Vermont. My parents are spending the first of several winters in Key West. Mother's letters are filled with news. At that time, it is a severely depressed town that has lost its one industry, cigar making, to Cuba. It is warm and cheap. The Roosevelt Administration has adopted it as a sort of foundling. The FERA (Federal Emergency Relief Administration) is promoting tourism, commissioning artists to do murals in the cafes, subsidizing theater, a fiesta, the "Semana Allegra," in an effort to keep the town afloat. Every few days someone pops down from Washington with a new plan for Key West including a "free port!" "Key

West is pretty free as it is; gambling open and widespread, smuggling of liquor and other things, people do about as they please—driving around with last year's license plates or none at all! . . . Also a deal of rumba dancing (forbidden by law)." The following year they will return despite hurricane damage which has washed away bridges and causeways that gave access from the mainland. Five hundred families have been forced to leave because their jobs on the freight boats going to Havana are gone. "The FERA is still doing some things, but the gleam of hope and gayety is gone. It is practically a ghost town, everything failing and fading," Mother writes.

As yet there are few tourists, and it "still has a pleasant shanty-town look." Edward Bruce, a painter and head of the Federal Arts Project, under which artists are hired to paint murals in public buildings, and his wife, Peggy, spend a few winters there. The place is attracting artists and writers. Ernest Hemingway and his wife, Pauline, own a house. Mother describes a visit to them:

"It is an old Spanish house of stone and cement, with balconies of wrought iron round both stories and long arched French windows all round—right in the middle of town near the lighthouse. . . . Their beautiful living room has heads of game that Ernest killed, stuck up all round . . . an enormous moose nearly fills an end wall, and there are a number of gazelles, etc. along the sides and on the floor a huge lion skin with head and feet all complete. I feel the room would be nicer without these, as it has lovely Spanish furniture and some interesting pictures. . . . Ernest was lounging in a large

chair in the living room. . . . He is simply enormous! He looks heavy and has lost his youthful
good looks, but still has his flashing, vivid smile
and engaging boyish quality. . . . We talked about
the old days. He remembered all you children and
especially Miriam." She tells him that I think *A
Farewell to Arms*, recently published, is the best
novel I have ever read, at which "he smiled with
pleasure, looking very handsome and said: 'Miriam
is prejudiced! I can think of four that are just as
good as that!' "

In her recently published *Autobiography of Alice
B. Toklas* Gertrude Stein has said some hard things
about Hemingway. "He talked a long time, quite
passionately about that, how surprised and hurt he
was, as he thought they were good friends and he
had liked her and got her things published here,
and had taught her to write dialogue; and then she
goes and knifes him. . . . He and Father had a
grand anvil chorus knocking Gertie."

Father and Leo, Gertrude's brother, had been
friends since the 1890s, and both my parents had
liked Gertrude and seen much of her in Italy and
Paris. They had made many attempts to find a publisher for her first book, *Three Lives*. But, as also
was the case with Mabel Dodge, who in 1913 with
publication of "A Portrait of Mabel Dodge at the
Villa Curonia" first brought Gertrude to public
notice, she tended to turn on those who had assisted her on the way to "*la gloire*." She and Leo,
who had been very close and had lived together in
Paris where they patronized the young artists
Matisse and Picasso, were friends no longer. He
considered her writing nonsense and once wrote Fa-

ther: "When Jesus said 'Verily, verily,' he was interesting. But if he had said, 'Verily, verily, verily, verily,' someone would have yelled, 'We've heard that before.'" In 1928 Father took me to her house in Paris. There were other people there gathered around her as she sat enthroned, it seemed to me, on a raised dais.

Next time you come, Pauline tells my parents, come to the side or tradesman's entrance as we have to lock the front gate. "It must be terrible to be a lion," Mother writes. At a party given by Carlo Tresca, "an old syndicalist and labor agitator," who is gay and charming, cooks spaghetti and meatballs and hires a Cuban orchestra, Ernest does "a bullfighter's stunt very gracefully, waving a coat." A few years later Tresca is assassinated in New York.

Father's correspondence with Dreiser is published in the *Nation* under headline "Is Dreiser Anti-Semitic?" It creates a furore. "The whole East Side is humming like a hive! . . . All the Yiddish papers carry long articles . . . Cahan says everyone is talking about it; and the letters certainly make Dreiser look like a fool! . . . the regular papers are terribly afraid of the Jewish question," Mother writes.

In the spring we set out in our car—now a sedan—on the 2,000-mile trip to Taos. A baggage trailer carries Ned's paraphernalia. We are many days on the road for we must stop early each day at a "tourist home"—a private house that rents rooms—unload Ned's crib, bathinette, and potty chair, wash diapers, prepare his food, and get him to sleep before finally falling into bed ourselves. A snapshot of me feeding Ned his lunch by the side of the road shows me thin and haggard. In Indiana we will pick up a friend, Mary Jane Woolsey, who will spend the summer and help me with the baby.

Once more as we cross the Great Plains we witness the devastation of the Dust Bowl era, later brought so vividly to life in John Steinbeck's agonizing tale, *The Grapes of Wrath*. The road is straight over the flat land, except where suddenly it turns at a right angle to avoid a farmer's field, barren without a trace of green. Scattered farmhouses seem empty and lifeless. Wind lifts the dry soil filling the air, darkening the sun; it sifts through the floor of the car. We wear wet cloths across nose and mouth. Huge billboards with Biblical texts convey a people's despair.

But in Wilson Point, even in Provincetown, we are shielded from the worst aspects of the depression. Many of our friends living in New York or other cities are seeing day-by-day the destitute, the apple sellers, who, not long ago, were earning good wages or salaries and are suddenly without a dime. Accounts of strikes, violence and misery fill the metropolitan newspapers. Moved by the plight of millions and in reaction to the rise of the right-wing dictators, Hitler, Mussolini and Franco, many move to the left. Hemingway and John Dos Passos, who go to Spain to observe the war, embrace the Republican cause. Surprisingly, given his reformist past, Lincoln Steffens becomes a Communist. My young cousin, Charles Boyce, is killed in Spain fighting with the Abraham Lincoln Brigade against Franco. My brother, carried away by the noble rhetoric of Communism, tries in vain to convert my father, who, however, takes a more philosophical view. In several letters he states his position. He is willing, he tells Charles, "for the world to assume any social or political form that will moderate and lessen the sum-total of human misery. But I feel that the world already has certain things that are good . . . incorporated in our present status are some measure of freedom of thought, speech and activity . . . that is very precious . . . If, by the exercise of great patience, it is possible to improve adequately our economic difficulties, there is less danger, I think, of losing our individual freedom, with all its resulting cultural goods, than by any form of absolute governmental control. I am certainly conservative in the sense that I feel deeply the culture of the past and do not want it sacrificed." Our revolutionists, he believes, "need to learn to use our words and to allow any principle to grow out of an intense understanding of local conditions." Mother writes: "I don't think it's worth any great sacrifice to put the Proletariat on top." We are in a revolution now, she thinks. The way we Americans proceed is to kick for years, and when there are enough kickers, the change takes place.

There is often bitter argument between the Left and those, like Father, who are "liberals." Mother recounts a dinner in New York with Arthur Garfield Hayes, well-known head of the American Civil Liberties Union: "Battle raged all evening between the Communist and Democratic points of view, but without bloodshed. Hayes and Father stood shoulder-to-shoulder for our old traditional liberties and individualism, Hayes saying he would not surrender any measure of liberty that he now has in the expectation of getting it back again some day, but would fight to the death for the freedom of the individual and what he wanted was more democracy."

As a child I listened to the arguments around our dinner table of my parents' friends, some of them Anarchists, Socialists, Communists, or Liberals, for Father was interested in hearing all points of view, especially of those more or less rejected by society. I suppose I absorbed, without being aware, much of Father's attitude. Although I have not thought deeply about politics, it is my natural tendency to look at both sides of a question and thus to settle somewhere between them. I am becoming more interested in the broader world as the picture darkens. But Taos is a Shangri-La, isolated, difficult of access, a place complete in itself. Brett, from England, sees it constantly before her eyes, "a shimmer of joy and beauty." Edward and I, once there, become intent on our own little problems and pleasures; we do not grasp at the time the immensity of the disaster that has overtaken the country and the world.

Life is amusing; the gossip is colorful. The latest is the recently constructed tomb of Lawrence at the ranch on the Lobo. I write Trix: "Angelino built it of cement on top of a hill, with a rose window by Brett. The walls are blue polka dots on a white ground . . . a sort of altar and rail and guest book stand—horribly done by Harry Simms—and a plaster of paris phoenix over the altar by Angelino! Frieda's daughter, Barbara, arrived on the scene and made a terrible row, and the upshot was that she and Brett did it over and now it is worse . . . silver radiator paint, primrose yellow and blue inside . . . and a pink door with buffaloes . . . a tin phoenix perched on the roof! Angelino says it looks like the ten-cent store, and of course he is terribly mad because Barbara and her husband (although Frieda paid their passage over and they are her guests) are trying their best to oust Angelino and get the ranch away from him. They tell Frieda he doesn't love her and is only after her money, etc. So you can imagine how pleasant it is there! Poor Frieda! Finally she asks them to leave. 'If you will divorce your husband you can stay on here,' she tells Barbie."

Among the visiting celebrities are Edna Ferber and Thomas Wolfe. Wolfe is slated to stay at Mabel's, for she likes his book, but he doesn't show up. "Finally he called from Santa Fe to say he would arrive at 11 A.M. the following day. At 9 P.M. the following day he called from Taos to say he would be up in half an hour. At 9:30 Mabel went to bed—having, however, his room ready and two lady visitors to receive him. He arrived at last very drunk with two women and when he heard Mabel had gone to bed he was furious. So he looked at one of Mabel's guests—a very dignified person—and said 'What's that old bitch doing here?' and to the other—a young woman—'You snore, I know you do.' There followed a stream of invective and he left, and yet he is very popular and they say very sweet when sober.

"Maurice Sterne was here just for a day, and went to lunch at Mabel's, and we were there. . . . He was very embarrassed and so was Mabel, and Tony never showed up. (He objected violently in the first place to Maurice coming and Mabel explained that it was 'only civilized' and the way white people do things. But Tony only said 'Indians don't do such things.') And Maurice made a good many truculent remarks in a loud voice, such as (speaking of an Indian in Santa Fe) 'He's the only Indian I ever liked.' They had a Swiss psychoanalyst with them who wants to start a very small and select insane asylum here!" Mary Jane is to leave soon which means "I will be chained to my post again. Mabel has asked us to spend a month with her when the cold sets in as she gets lonely in the winter."

By Christmas, after a pleasant few weeks with Mabel, we are back in our own house and have hired a maid for five dollars a week, which is a dollar more than the going rate. She is my beloved Margaret, the beautiful daughter of a Mexican family in Ranchos de Taos. Her mother, known as "Grandma," climbs ladders and tierra blancas our walls once a year. Margaret has married an Anglo, Sam Davidson, and has two small boys. But he has become ill with t.b. of the hip bone and they are desparate for money. She works for me for a year or so and then on and off through my years in Taos. Eventually, the t.b. is cured, though he remains a cripple, and they are able to buy a house in Santa Fe. She is as meaningful in my life as are other close friends; we keep in touch for many years. Poor Margaret! One of her sons is later killed in an accident and there is some kind of trouble with the other. But by then there are grandchildren to engage her love. Later, her sister-in-law, Teodula, comes often to look after the children while I am skiing. She, too, is beautiful. While Margaret resembles a gentle Madonna, Teodula has the features and bearing of an enigmatic goddess. Both come from dirt-poor families in Ranchos de Taos, both are dignified, admirable women.

Margaret's presence gives me more freedom and we drive up the mountain to where the snow is deep. A ski run has been opened with a log cabin lodge, a rope tow and a Swiss instructor. I become enamored; the feeling as of flying; the snowy slopes and woods; the pure, sunlit air; the excitement of a straight run and then the successful turn at the finish. I ski whenever I possibly can during my remaining years in Taos.

Following the Christmas ceremonies at the turn of the year, as the sun begins its slow migration and the lengthening days give hope of rebirth, is Twelfth Night, the time when Pueblo officers are inaugurated. The new officers open their houses to troops of singers and dancers. By special invitation we watch, sitting on adobe benches around the walls of a pueblo lodging. The Indian men crouch on their heels, impassive and unmoving, women hold babies in their arms, voices are quiet and low. Suddenly there is the sound of bells, the door flies open, several singers with a drum and then the dancers appear. The musicians are wrapped in blankets, the bodies of the dancers are painted, their costumes witty; one has a tail. They are accomplished performers, their dances satirical and funny. At the end of their act, the women reward them with cakes and bread. Then they are gone and we await the next. "We see about a dozen groups," I write my parents. "Some are tiny boys and girls dressed in feathers, an eagle dance . . . a gliding with eagle wings, a lot of clowns with masks, a

squaw dance . . . and such a warm, friendly, se-
rene, jolly atmosphere!" Although the Taos Indian
is poor by our standards, he seems fortunate.
Bound together by tradition and myth constantly
renewed in his festivals and dances, he retains a
sense of community with his pueblo and with nature. His life seems to have meaning as part of an
all-embracing scheme. It is this that has drawn
Mabel to Tony and the Indians.

It is the three distinct cultures—Indian, Mexican
and that of the Old West—and Taos the place—that
attract the artists and writers and hold us all; it is
the high desert air, the light, the intense color, the
huge cloud shadows moving across the mountains,
the sunset glow for which the Sangre de Cristo
range is named. This high valley ringed by mountains envelops us all. Famous people who are drawn
here—and there are many—come under its spell.
Robinson and Una Jeffers come often; Aldous Hux-
ley spends a summer on the Lobo; Mabel's old
friends from New York pass through: Margaret
Sanger on her way to China for "the Cause,"
Frances Perkins, the Secretary of Labor. They bring
their insights, add their dimension, but do not
stand apart—their greatness becomes a part of our
lives, our experience of Taos. Upon our idyll more
and more via radio, and a few subscriptions to the
New York Times, which takes three days to reach us,
the outside world obtrudes. I hear from Brett, who
is visiting her family in England, buying herself
kilts and a velvet kilt coat and has ordered a kilt for
me. In a somewhat patronizing tone she tells me
that England is astonished by "American hysteria"
over war danger. In October 1935 Italy has attacked

and later conquers Ethiopia, the League of Nations swallows the *fait accompli* in the hope of keeping Mussolini on their side to restrain Hitler, and German troops enter the Rhineland, a demilitarized zone, but England continues blindly to hope for the best.

Closer to home there is family news. Trix is having a hard time. She and the baby are still on Long Island with the Fausts, while Luke is hunting for an apartment in Bridgeport where he has a job reporting for the *Times Star*. Bridgeport is booming because of the Remington Arms factory, which is supplying American and European demand.

Following Roosevelt's election by a landslide to a second term, at the end of 1936, American attention is distracted from ominous events on the continent and riveted on the romantic story unfolding in England and the abdication of King Edward VIII. I listen, as do millions of others, to his abdication speech in which he declares that he is forsaking the Crown "for the woman I love." I see it as a human tragedy in the classic sense, that is, when the hero's fatal flaw leads inevitably to his doom. Mother agrees: "Yes, it is a tragedy. For one thing, Edward can't get out of the white light that beats upon a throne, even by leaving it. He can't be an ordinary citizen. And now he is defenseless. . . . He must feel as though he has been skinned. Royal people are protected as long as they stay in power. . . . The poor man has no place to go. It will be like the Lindbergh persecution, perhaps worse. And then the woman is problematic . . . and no woman can really make up to a man for giving up his whole way of living and what career he has, even if he thinks he wants to get rid of it. He seems to be a type that is unhappy anyhow. But I agree with you that he is appealing, that his speech was a wonderful and moving one—I'm afraid he is a poet and will have a hard time of it." She has had a stormy letter from Eva Cruikshank, a Britisher, sympathetic with the working class into which she was born, who is furious with him for quitting. She has been hanging on the radio for weeks, weeping floods, and her American husband doesn't know what is the matter with her. The *New Yorker* is moved to publish a piece entitled "To the King Over the Water." Americans seem more sympathetic to the king than the British people. Mother is disappointed. "I had visions of the people rising and storming the Houses of Parliament—but no, they have lost their King without a murmur. . . . Two things I am sore about—one that they didn't let him keep his Duchy of Cornwall, where Tristan and Iseult loved—that is the setting for their love-story! . . ." and "it was said that he would sail on the yacht *Enchantress*—another nice touch. But what do they do? send him off on the warship *Fury*!!!"

Though life for me is full of interest, Edward more and more retreats into an unknown world. He is not really immersed in his work, he does not pay much attention to Ned, who by now is a handsome little boy, he spends much time at the hotel playing chess. I have so much else in my life that most of the time I am content, but I do feel his absence as a father and a companion. Mother and Mabel enjoy his quiet, undemanding presence, and I think that if he had been occupied with something that really interested him, I would have been satisfied in spite of the absence of any real communication. In a way, he seems to be living through me, not giving much back to life. And that does not satisfy him either. Ned, Margaret and I are only the backdrop, the scene against which his soliloquy is played.

Mother enjoys Edward because as she says, "He doesn't stir up a FUSS about things. But his big frame moves around so easily and quietly, he never makes any disturbance in a house. There is a kind of elegance about his motions, he never BOUNCES. If he likes to exist within himself a good part of the time, not impinging on other people, why not? I could never understand why people, like Hutch, should get so irritated with others, like me and Edward, who just soak things in and maybe mull over them inside, and then perhaps express them in our own way and perhaps not!" And she contrasts Father, "Who doesn't get a bit quieter with age and when he is here in this little quiet house . . . why the place simply rocks and trembles. He is an earthquake, that's what he is, an Act of God! And to think that I should get him who have always liked a quiet life!" My father, who is a very social being, is often irritated by Mother's desire for solitude and quiet, but unlike Edward, she is deeply interested in life, there is something creative going on within her which she expresses in action—in writing, gardening, hooking rugs or in some other fashion. In Edward, on the other hand, there seems to be something blocking his expression and his interest. He seems to be escaping or blotting out the world. He often retires into the living room where he plays Ravel's "Bolero" over and over and over again. As time goes on, when he paints he scrapes off the canvas before anyone has a chance to look at it. He does not finish a painting.

My very different parents needed each other's qualities. Mother's tragic childhood—the deaths of four brothers and sisters in a typhoid epidemic, the deaths of other close relatives and friends, and her subsequent lonely childhood on a ranch in California—left her afraid of intimacy, intensifying her natural reserve. By his persistence, Father was able to break through the barrier; he was a goad, a constant source of irritation and stimulation. With a philosophical turn of mind, a gift of expression, his thoughts constantly fermenting and bubbling to the surface, he stirred her up, brought her into contact with new people and enlarged what might have been a narrower existence. She says in a letter, "Things always seem very slow and empty without you around. Life without you is stale, flat and unprofitable."

At the same time, Father has a deep need of Mother. In a letter to Mabel he refers to himself as a "cripple" in the same sense in which she is a "cut flower." That is, lacking a deep faith in or connection with life. Mother, skeptical or even cynical as she sometimes seems, has that faith. "To me life is all positive—a passionate affirmation," she had written Mabel a year after her son Boyce's death. "With effort and struggle we must affirm and create. . . . Joy has a place and pain—they are to me both positive realities. But this world is a magnificent one—it overwhelms me often by its vastness, its splendor, its heroic quality. All its lives and colors are on a vast and brilliant scale. It takes effort to live in it . . . but it is the only place I can live in now. No, I haven't reached the plane you speak of, where I am at home in such a world. I am a bewildered pilgrim! But I can see that it is glorious."

By contrast, Father writes to Mabel about *Movers and Shakers*, her new volume of *Intimate Memories:* "The picture of yourself, your striving, unhappy self, more unhappy even than you know—restlessly striving to make up for an original lesion—which separated you from the life of nature—from the life of human nature. Did it happen in your childhood, or through a higher Providence that wished the creative results of your misfortune? . . . conscious of the beauty, peculiarly conscious of the beauty the source of which had been withdrawn. Hence your . . . intense hunches . . . your flashes of insight. You couldn't quietly dwell with it, for it wasn't there. . . . Perhaps that is the bond that is really between us. . . . You have the same sympathetic understanding of me as I have of you—perhaps because we are both cripples! I in my way, you in yours." Mother and Tony have an unconscious, unquestioning acceptance of life while Father and Mabel are always searching for the eternal—the Why.

My parents' marriage lasted because they both understood the bond that held them. A postscript to a letter written to me on Ned's second birthday conveys something of the enjoyment they had of each other, "P.S. . . . on the day Snooks was two years old, your mother and I had been married thirty-seven years. And we put the two girls to bed early that night, and we supped all alone on two of the best lobsters that I have ever known and a bottle of champagne that was of the best, lovely lettuce from our own garden to go with the lobster. Then we had a very gay talk, in firelight and candle-light, in the truly French style, underlying which was a slight vein of Anglo-Saxon weight to give the lightness more direction. It reminded me of some of the best comedies of Schnitzler, indeed it was somewhat similar to those witty things that happen in the *cabinets particuliers* of Gallic life. Our imaginations went back thirty-seven years, and our amused memories through many intervening times, especially in Europe, about the time you were born, when we were so much entertained by association with the Algar Thorolds, and other really serious people who were putting on a light front. In other words we had a very good time, and it reminded us of times when we were young, also brought to mind the happy thought that we are still young!"

Many of his friends have said that Father raised the quality of feeling in those around him. He certainly did it for me. Although he sometimes irritated me or embarrassed me in public by his unconventionality, I enjoyed his company. About this time I wrote him that I wished he and I could go off on a jaunt. "I always have such a good time with you when I get you off alone, away from family worries."

Although more like Father in temperament, I, like Mother, seem to be the one with the strong connection to life and I the one called upon to supply it. For a number of years, adding to and rebuilding a house, making a garden, furniture, painting and fathering children, belonging to a family of his own, seems, with some lapses, to satisfy Edward. But as time goes on, these lapses become more frequent and prolonged and he retreats deeper and deeper into—who knows what world. "He is very dependent on you for his life-interest . . . some thing happened to him to choke that life-impulse . . . I suppose if he lost you, he would revert to his Sandwich state." Mother truly foresees.

In one of these periods when he is virtually not there, our marriage is severely strained. I am questioning not only my feelings about Edward but also myself, my courage, my principles, my basis of belief. In my search, I turn to my parents for guidance. To Father I write: "I have been thinking of you a great deal lately and of what a remarkably good person you are and how much you really love everyone—and wish you would tell me what your principles are! I have always thought I had strong principles or standards but I find they were much too simple and would only survive as long as I wasn't faced with any real problems—I now find myself completely at sea. I have always been led to believe by you and Mother and have always considered myself a fundamentally nice person—but now I am not at all sure. I find I am egotistical and vain to an extraordinary degree—I hope it is natural but am afraid not. And I don't like people as much as I did—I see their faults so clearly. One thing is I have never really done anything for myself—it has all been done for me—and I don't mean materially only, I have been extraordinarily well protected not only by my parents but by my friends! Which is in many ways a great disadvantage—especially if one

realizes that it cannot and must not go on forever—
but every way—and so I have never found out
about myself and my principles." This wrestling
with myself continues throughout my life as I focus
on one side or the other. Beneath it there is a
strong foundation laid down in childhood, a sense
of obligation as well as the feeling that life is for
living, feeling and expression.

Father replies: "Your very appreciative letter
pleased me greatly but at the same time made me
feel very hypocritical, knowing in my inner self
that I could honestly accept only a fragment of it.
In that respect you and I are very much alike, you
are even more unwilling than I am to accept anything good in yourself. You have always been even
rather morbidly self-critical, very conscientious. I
don't think it is because of any definite principles,
such as you speak of, but of a strong desire to be
right, and that is so specific and complex that principles are at best but vague sign-posts dimly appear-
ing in the mist. It is a pilgrim's progress for all of
us, and I suppose the really good thing is to be consciously determined on finding the path.

"About myself, I do not really love everyone as
you say. I see great differences of value, and how in
comparison some are lovable and some are not. But
when I think philosophically rather than socially I
do attribute a necessary value to every living thing.
The organism of life has a value to me which is so
strong that it may fairly be said to be infinite as an
expression of the superlative. I really think this
feeling in me is the best that I have and that in
some way, although entirely untheological, it is yet
religious.

"You evidently want some guiding principles, and seem to desire me to express to you my principles. Whenever I am conscious of principles, I am conscious of them only because they bear upon the essential respect for other people, derived from my mystic feeling for their value. If every living person is a child of God, he is surely worthy of our love and respect. The seemingly little matter of keeping an engagement is something that I have felt very strongly all my life; for to miss one without absolute necessity is a sign if not of contempt for the other person, at least of putting his welfare in a place not inferior to your own. We are all of us selfish, in that we necessarily look at things from the point of view of our own personal consciousness; for this is the only way that we can look at them; but to keep our understanding and contracts with others is all-important, socially because without that human society cannot hold together, and morally because not doing so means religious blindness—to the value of other created things.

"This is a simple statement, but in action the factors of which are always complex, it is always a problem to be sure, because of the necessary habitual conflicts. That is why at the best our path is always that of Bunyan's hero, and as long as we are following it strenuously we are doing our best. It is only when we cease to try that we have yielded to what is called the devil.

"I hope you always feel about me as you do now and that we can have many talks about this great subject."

After the years of pregnancy, Ned's birth and two years of dedication to motherhood, I have suddenly emerged from that phase of my life. The suddenness of the change, though this time not from depression, parallels the change five years before when I come to Taos and is as much of a surprise to me as it is to my parents. Precipitating the change is the appearance in Taos of a young man, much younger than I am, who attaches himself to me, haunts our house, which he has leisure to do as he works as night clerk in a local hotel, and calls me at night. He is good-looking, intelligent, lively and amusing. We have fun together. I shed my serious, conscientious side like a cocoon and become a butterfly tasting the sweets of male admiration. It is as if I am two different persons—on the surface—for there remains a fundamentally serious attitude toward obligations.

An important contributing factor is Edward's usual lack of attention. He chooses this time to absent himself completely, first by spending most of the summer at Frieda's, then by going east for a month. While there, he pays a visit to my parents in Richmond. Though he is not one to talk, he looks unhappy and does say that I am "going through a period of unusual gaiety." Mother senses something is wrong, writes Mabel, and this precipitates a flurry of letters. Mother worries that Mabel has stirred up trouble over Frieda. "I know there is nothing between her and Edward except mutual stimulation," I reply. "As a matter of fact I was very pleased at his staying there most of the summer—because I was glad to be alone—and to have some fun and some life free from the burden of worry about Edward and annoyance at his complete lack of vitality and interest in anything. You know I really love Edward and I agree with everything you say about him—but he has gone absolutely dead. And he is going to take me that way too unless I put up a strong resistance. I want to live—perhaps it's only selfishness. But anyway I want it—I want to be in the world—of ideas and movements and with people who are doing things. . . . The only hope for him is a terrific outside stimulus . . . going South with you would be only a very pleasant evasion of the issues. You may think this change in me is too sudden to be serious—but I don't think it is sudden. It simply came to a head suddenly because I met a man who stimulated and amused me and made me begin to think and be conscious of things that have been brewing in me for some time. If it hadn't been for the baby it would have come much sooner. Ned is a wonderful, darling child and I'm deeply glad I have him. And don't think I'm really unhappy—I have serious problems to face but I'd rather be doing that than nothing at all. Kiss darling Pa for me and thank him for his very angelic letter. He is the sweetest person who ever lived. And you are the next!"

Mother replies to both my letters: "It doesn't seem to me a matter of 'principles' that you need to settle, but of deep desire, it is a question of finding out what you really want most. Often when we think we have settled our lives in accordance with what we want, chance desires will cut across the current and for the time being deflect us and we think we have mistaken our real direction and must follow a new impulse. I remember discussing that with Mabel once, and she said that temperamental desire was the whole thing and meant life and one must follow it—as of course she was then doing and always has. But I said no, it might pass very soon and unless it was simply experience you were after, no matter what kind, the result would be disappointment and losing your bearings generally. Your temperamental desire now is for experience with other men, 'Life,' you say; and of course you should have as much social life and experience with people as you can swing—but not on principle or because you owe it to yourself! as a lot of women think. And it's only a tough-shelled person like Mabel who can go on acquiring and shedding relationships throughout life without turning a hair, so to speak! For a sensitive person, every intimate relationship takes something out, as well as giving something, and isn't easy to break. And when it conflicts with what you already have the nervous strain is intense and may break one down—But that has to be worked out, on the basis of what you really deeply want to keep in your life, then fitting in minor interests if and when possible." Mother, herself, has experienced this conflict many years ago shortly after my birth, when she was faced with choosing between her husband and family and another man.

Mabel tries to reassure my parents but only succeeds in making them suspicious of her. She to Father: "I never have seen her looking better or happier and for the first time she seems in possession of herself and poised. She has a beau and you know how that sets one up. Really one needs beaux in those early years, especially those gay boys who have no vocation in life other than to be very quick on the uptake, amusing and full of beans. . . .

[Edward] is the silentest thing I ever saw and I don't know what is going on inside him. His best quality to my mind is his sort of dependability. . . . Miriam will not lose such a security as this easily for she likes and needs it. . . . Edward never 'acts the father' and this annoys her. But Edward just can't fill any of these familiar parts and never will. Yet queerly enough I miss him when he is away. He is something, no matter how odd and unsatisfactory or how seemingly unconcerned and unsocial. He seems sometimes like someone from another planet. (Even Edward's mother agrees that her son is a complete original and not like anybody else in the world . . .) Of course Miriam wants someone from this planet." She advises Father to let it be. "She has a sagacious upper lip that indicates common sense, and she thinks things out," she says.

But my parents are afraid I will throw everything overboard for Arch. They think Mabel is encouraging me and that, much as they appreciate her personal qualities, she is often a destructive influence. Not for the first time, Father expresses regret that he bought me the house in Taos. There is no doubt she has had a powerful influence, perhaps in some ways bad in that she is an example of a woman who experiments freely with all kinds of relationships and with her resilience and financial independence has managed to come through to what seems like a satisfactory conclusion. On the other hand, if I had not settled in Taos think of how much I would have missed of that wonderful world which she played a large part in opening up to me! "I really know that my feeling for Arch is not the real thing, nor is his for me; he is obviously a playboy. My giddy reaction to his attentions, my impulse to kick up my heels, is perhaps a manifestation of late adolescence or an act of desperation, to escape from the close confines of my secure cage. Eventually a tough world will force me into adulthood. But Mabel's insight does not err when she warns me that dallying with Arch will change my feeling for Edward, make me more critical.

Several factors contribute to the crisis. John Evans's first wife, Alice, a designer and owner of a dress shop in Santa Fe, asks me to be a model in a fashion show to be held in Taos. Her original and beautiful garments captivate me and I am able to acquire a canary yellow corduroy coat, a cocktail gown and a skirt, shorts and halter of red bandanas. Since the time when, as a little girl, I dressed up in my mother's clothes, dress has been a real passion with me, perhaps reflecting the frivolous side of my nature. Consciousness of being well and appropriately dressed has had an important bearing on my self-esteem, which in turn affects my mood and my attractiveness. In periods when my confidence is at a low ebb, I become a different person; this has happened several times in my life. When I attract favorable regard, especially masculine admiration, I respond by becoming vivacious, prettier and more appealing. Clothes do not "make the man" or woman. But a well-chosen garment, a new and becoming hat can make a woman feel more attractive, boosting her confidence, and hence becoming more so. Moreover, clothes are fun. Nothing sets one up like a new hat! "It is a terribly risky thing . . . to play with other men. . . . There are certain fundamental differences between the two sexes, which makes to the male the so-called freedom of the female, the absolute negation of all good between them; it will take a few million years of propaganda and of control of the instincts to make it fundamentally different." I am demanding a great sacrifice from Edward "which will call for him not really to feel . . . for a woman there is only one mate at a time." I agree with this last as I am naturally monogamous and conservative in that way. Actually my brief and unsatisfactory sexual adventure with Arch did not take place until Edward had absented himself for most of the summer. Arch leaves in the fall for New York and that puts the effective finish. After reading a letter from Arch to Mabel, Mother writes: "Neither of us like that boy. Sort of a 'wind-blow'—the apples that fall off the tree before they are ripe and are rotten to the core."

My parents misjudge my seriousness and also blame Mabel unfairly for what they believe is her encouragement. She actually interfered to discourage the affair. I think it is true, as she writes Father, that it would change my feelings for Edward, make me more critical of him. And I think she was right; it gave me a taste of a different kind of interchange and it damaged Edward's shaky self-esteem, though we did come close again for a while.

There are illness, trouble and discord in our personal lives. Edward, always a loner, inscrutable, becomes remote. Little by little he drifts off into a world apart from mine and from the childrens'. Eventually, long absent in spirit, he removes himself physically from Taos. Eventually, we too must leave. But in the intense light of recollection, the shadows fade and leave only the shining moment. It is a time deeply imprinted, a time to remember, a discrete small world, in which time and space combine to create something unique and evanescent as a bubble vanishing with the tide of history.

AFTERWORD
by Edward Hapgood Bright

Naturally children are different from their parents,
but they are also impressionable, and essential attitudes are conveyed, parent to child. I mean in this
Afterword to tell what became of a few of the people introduced in this book, but particularly to show
how Miriam's story, my mother's story, unfolded
after she left Taos. I take after her in many ways,
probably in more ways than I know, but at the
same time I am much removed from her. In telling
her story, I have tried to characterize her and I have
found the task surprisingly difficult. The difficulty
is that although I am like her, I do not own her
eyes, her mind or her sympathies. A faint bitter-
ness debilitates my sympathies and I am cynical in
a way which she never was. Despite life's vicissi-
tudes, she possessed always an essential optimism.
A simple and indestructible enthusiasm permitted
her to recover and again enjoy both people and that
natural world that lies beyond the bounds of human order and control.

My mother came to write her memories of Taos
in large part because of an accident. Of course she
intended to write them one day, for it is a necessity

for many in their old age to try and reckon where they have been in the wandering course of a lifetime. But it was accident that propelled her to fulfill her good intentions and actually get down to writing. Picking beach plums one day from the wild bushes on her Provincetown, Massachusetts place, she scratched an eye. This insult set in train a reaction, an inflammation of the muscles behind the eye. Before her Graves Disease was correctly diagnosed and controlled, the swollen muscles behind both eyes had pinched the optic nerves which pass between them and damaged her vision. On account of damaged vision she thenceforward concentrated much less of her energy on her painting and a great deal more on her writing. Now eighty years old and keeping house alone in Provincetown, she drove herself on to do a great many things, brushing aside with difficulty the tiresome companion of old age, fatigue. She kept on producing and showing art, though with reduced vision this now often took the form of collages made out of painted blocks of wood. The three-dimensional wood shapes she could see well enough and manipulate.

It was ironic, she remarked, that the first really disabling blow to fall upon her should damage her eyes. She lived through her eyes.

My mother planned to recollect her entire life in one large memoir, but in the end she finished and polished only fraction of the whole, the part published here. She died suddenly in April 1990, in Boston, at age 84, of a progressive lung inflammation which the doctors neither understood nor could control. She took to the Boston hospital notes for further pages she intended to add to her recollection here of Taos.

When she died she had been retired to Provincetown, Massachusetts, for some years and had found a niche in this pleasant town on the Atlantic shore. Here she once roamed freely as a small child over sand beach and dune and in the picturesque streets running along the harbor front, which then smelled of drying fish and the wood tar that proofed the drying trawler nets. Obituaries described her as an environmental activist, a "fighter" who battled for environmental protection and for curtailed development in Provincetown. An obituary writer reported a friend as saying: "She was very sensitive to the environment. She wouldn't even kill a mouse."

Since retiring to Provincetown in 1977 with her third husband, John DeWitt, she had written sheaves of Letters to the Editor, organized with others local protest and pressure, written a newspaper column on environmental issues and testified often at board hearings and at Town Meeting. A reporter for the *Cape Codder* recalled that in an interview published in the paper she had said: "What I see is very important to me. Having known Provincetown when it was just a small, beautiful fishing village, I get very upset about what has happened here. We just can't support any more development in this town. I don't know why people don't understand that." In a letter of her own to a friend some years before, she wrote, "Provincetown isn't the same town it was in our youth." "I swear I won't get involved in any more hopeless crusades and then I find myself so outraged that I have to fire another shot."

She had many years before been instrumental with others in plucking a large tract of land behind the town from the grasp of would-be local developers and their cronies in the Massachusetts State bureaucracy. The activists succeeded in preserving this considerable tract, an original land grant called the Provincelands, for inclusion in the then-tentative, but now well-established Cape Cod National Seashore Park. One obituary writer noted that more recently she had been active in the movement to preserve eighteen dune shacks in the Park behind Provincetown. These had been built before the arrival of the Park and inhabited every summer since. These nourish the creative spirit, my mother had said, for in the shacks life is simplified and one lives away from distraction and close to nature. For my mother, Nature was indeed nourishing (and therefore worth protecting). Her paintings, nearly always of some natural subject, are evidence of the nutritive value it held for her, as I believe this word picture of the dunes themselves shows: "There are groves of stunted trees in the hollows, bogs where tiny purple orchids grow next to scarlet fungi, and where cranberries in the fall glow crimson. The sand still marches relentlessly upon the forest, and traces of ancient trees emerge in clay ridges from some forgotten wetland."

At the end of her life, then, my mother was attempting to safeguard the very things she had come to appreciate during her years in Taos, a time when you might safely say she was politically unconscious. I believe that her visual sympathies were first expressed and first found reward in Taos. There was a nourishing magic there in the Taos Valley to be found in Nature and it was given entry through the eye. In any case she took away something from Taos when she left in 1942 to go to Washington, the federal capital and the administrative focus of the "war effort."

Mabel, I believe, was right when she wrote, in the Summer 1951 issue of the *New Mexico Quarterly*, of Taos in the decades before the War. "Those were the days!" Then "there was an exchange between people and the environment, each contributed to the other. . . . The "visitors and the magical earth had created together an influence, and the impact of one upon the other set up a chain reaction that continues. . . ."

Taos, where the environment was strong, does things to people, said Mabel. And people go away changed. Nature is designing and affects us, she suggested. We think that the universe is irrational and irresponsible, but, she intimated, perhaps it's the other way around. In any case, we are all unknowing. And without faith.

I think Taos Valley awakened in my mother a great sympathy for nature and a full responsiveness to the many living things in nature. She took this sympathy away with her. I believe it is what accounts for her persistence; her efforts over a lifetime both to represent in her painting and to protect by reasoned political process the source that nourishes both the human body and the human spirit.

As is evident from her memoir, my mother made and enjoyed many friends in Taos and she kept in

touch with them, particularly Spud Johnson, who
used to report all the news, and with Louie Cottam
and his daughter Barbara. But in Taos, as was more
plainly the case later, she had always to struggle to
balance many competing demands and interests.
She probably did as well as any modern woman to
negotiate the demands of her own projects and the
conflicting claims of others, near and far, upon her
attention and energy. She felt that she had been
successful in this respect in Taos, but not, of course,
successful in her marriage to Edward.

She left Taos in 1942 and went east, as Edward
had done the year before. But the two of them did
not get together again. Edward was in New York.
With only a few friends, one of whom was Paul
Strand, he kept mainly to himself. He lived in a
bachelor room rented at the Men's Residence Club
and found a job with a small contractor supplying
ranging and other instruments to the Army. Still a
very young lad, I visited him once in the city and
we went shopping. Returning me to my mother, he
complained that I had spent money like a drunken
sailor, but I have to own I was a greedy, materialis-
tic brat then. I have the letters, which he kept, that
I wrote to him while I was at school in Santa Fe. I
notice that in virtually every letter, I badgered him
to buy and send me a toy or some item.

He and my mother drifted apart. I got no mes-
sages from him except as conveyed at the ends of
letters to my mother. I have no letters from him
but many from his mother, who outlived him and
was quite attentive to his sons. Money which
passed to Tim and myself upon her death covered
my senior year expenses at Swarthmore College,

where I majored in political science. It paid Tim's way at the University of Virginia, where he studied fine arts. When I received the contents of Edward's room after he died, following a brief illness in 1954, I found that he kept framed photographs of myself and my brother with him. None of us attended his funeral, and a cousin on the Bright side saw to the arrangements. My mother saw him last in 1944 in New York to ask for a divorce. Up to that time, according to his brother, Bobby, he had not considered the possibility of a divorce. Bobby and my mother did maintain a friendly correspondence for many years. His brother was a good man, Bobby wrote, but destined never to understand affairs of the heart. Bobby and Katherine remained in the Taos Valley, and Bobby wrote children's books. Later they moved to Santa Fe, and after Katherine's death, Bobby moved to San Francisco, where his daughter Bebe also lived.

Arriving in the East not long after the outbreak of war, my mother plunged into a life spectacularly different from the one she had known in Taos. Her brother, Charles, who had a job with the Red Cross, and his wife, Tam, had managed to find a small apartment in Washington, D.C., despite an acute housing shortage there. Charles encouraged my mother to come to Washington, where jobs were plentiful, and he made room in his apartment for her to stay.

My mother, it is fair to say, had lived a privileged existence in Taos, where, admittedly, during the depression privilege cost very little. Now that she was in Washington, and effectively single, necessity demanded that she go to work immediately to support herself and her two boys. Having failed to finish her four years at Smith College, she lacked a degree. Her work experience was limited. Given her record, her prospects were not rosy. Fortunately however, the Washington job market was wide open. The times were heady ones. The city was just then being transformed. It was being made the administrative focus of America's vast preparations for global war. Thousands of people flocked to the federal capital (as they did to California and to Chicago and Detroit) to work in the war effort. It was a honor to serve in a great national cause, and women particularly were taken immediately into the labor force. Because of the nature of the emergency, the "raw recruits" were given great responsibilities. After working several months as a sales clerk in Jelleff's Department Store, my mother secured a position as Intelligence Clerk in the Bureau of Economic Warfare where she routed intercepted letters and cables to all sections of the Enemy Branch. Soon she moved to the position of Intelligence Officer in the Foreign Economic Administration. Here she prepared, for use after the war, reports on German industrial assets, particularly those of I. G. Farben, which had been smuggled to safe haven in neutral countries as insurance against a German defeat. Sources of information were extremely limited, she later noted, and principal reliance was placed on intercepted cable and postal traffic. "This work involved painstaking research and the exercise of specialized methods of analysis—necessitated by the fragmentary and often deliberately misleading character of the material."

A year later she was Executive Secretary of an

FEA Drafting Committee and as such helped to prepare a report which considered the pros and cons of separating the Ruhr-Rhineland Territory from Germany as a disarmament measure. In 1946 she held a position at the Office of War Mobilization and Reconversion. OWMR, she wrote in an application for federal employment some years later, acted as staff to the President on matters to do with converting the wartime economy to peacetime functioning after the war. As a Public Information Analyst she answered letters to President Truman querying national economic policy.

In 1943, after finding a tiny house for rent in a brand new government housing project, she was able to bring me to Washington to live with her. I had been lodged meantime first with the family of a school friend in Colorado, then with my mother's sister, Beatrix, in Connecticut. She brought Tim east in 1944 from a boarding school near Santa Fe, after finding and hiring Alameda to receive, feed and look after her two boys after school. Alamedas, who would mind one's home and one's children, were even harder to find then than a place for rent. For my mother, working virtually six days a week, Alameda was an essential of life.

The housing project was not a bad place for children. There were many of us in the place. We made friends and did things together, like explore the parkland that bordered the project on two sides. We played group games on the project's large lawns. Evidences that there was a war going on were indirect. A football or a new baseball glove was a scarce item. Victory gardens grew close to the project, which not only eased the shortage of fresh vegetables for some people, but on summer evenings provided gardeners and their families an escape from stifling apartments. (Washington, a southern city, did not then enjoy universal air conditioning.) My mother's work left her no time for her painting and little time for friends or for her boys. Yet she did revive old friendships like that with Agnes DeLano, an intelligent, cultivated woman who had been her teacher and friend at a preparatory school in Cambridge, Massachusetts. She made new friends of Chester and Orah Cooper, who would remain lifelong friends. And she met and fell in love with Vaso Trivanovitch.

Vaso, who worked for the Foreign Economic Administration, was a professional economist, a naturalized American citizen who had come to the United States from Yugoslavia when he was eighteen years old. When Vaso arrived, all three members of the family living in the tiny house in the housing project got at last the attention they craved.

My mother married Vaso in 1947 in Washington. In 1947 the new family moved to Armonk, N.Y. My mother got much interested in the United World Federalists at that time. Vaso worked for an export-import firm in New York City. In 1948 he was invited to join the faculty of Springfield College, the YMCA college in Springfield, Massachusetts, to teach economics. The family moved to Agawam, a suburb of Springfield, shortly after.

My mother's marriage to Vaso made good, in my opinion, the disappointments of her first marriage. Vaso's temperament was, first of all, very different from Edward's. Vaso had a Slav's temperament: warm and sturdy. He was a short, neat figure with a natural dignity. Except in politics, perhaps, he was conservative. His manners were old-fashioned even. My mother put a great value on manners. Manners were common courtesy which ought to be observed as ordinary social responsibility. It is the courtesies that give social interchange a little democratic grace. Lacking manners was not only lacking grace, but entirely contrary to American democratic spirit in her view. Manners were not instruments of oppression and phoney; rather they were guarantors of equality. In any case they were attractive in a person.

Vaso's sudden death of a heart attack in November 1949 broke my mother's heart and broke our freshly made family circle. Nature, now and for a long time after, yielded her no consolation, nothing. Nature was heedless and without feelings, stony and wooden. Only in human relations were there feelings—joy and grief. And:

> Grief is a long agony
> Endless yearning for what is gone
> Kisses tender and passionate
> The clasp of strong arms
> The warmth of his presence
> Which made the world
> Seem a kindly place.

She found work in Springfield, but as the wages were very low, she returned in due course to Washington in hopes of finding better paying employment. She did not find work there right away. And so she started in as a night school student at George Washington University to gain the remaining credits she needed to claim the degree she had failed to get at Smith College. She chose journalism as her major. After she had aggregated the required total of credits, George Washington duly awarded her a degree. This document, of course, made an impressive difference in her "earnings potential," but it is my belief that the prime benefit of the course work was to make her skillful in the use of the word and confident of its efficacy in politics. The exact word, like a painter's faultless image, could bleach distracting chimera to show the bony frame. She trusted a politician who spoke well. At least he or she must have a mind. She was certain that in a democracy there must be a necessary connection between political commentary/political criticism and practical political outcomes. Politics was in 1950 the art of the possible, not as now the art of misrepresentation. In due course her own environmentalist's politics would come out as literate argument in letters and testimony. What she appreciated, she would defend with the word.

In April 1951 she got a job as a Conference Writer in the Office of Price Stabilization. This was a federal agency created to deal with the economic effects of the Korean War. She got the work she needed to support herself and her two boys again in Washington. She was making a reasonable living from reasoned writing. A severe test of her belief in the reasoned word lay in store for her. For her as for thousands of others in the notorious fifties, the test arrived in this form (from the Regional Loyalty Board, January 1952):

As part of the process of determining your suitability for Federal Employment, an investigation has been conducted under the provisions of Executive Order 9835 as amended by Executive Order 10241, a copy of which is attached. This investigation disclosed information which, it is believed, you should have an opportunity to explain or refute.

[The standard for the refusal of employment or the removal from employment in an executive department or agency on grounds relating to loyalty shall be that, on all the evidence, there is a reasonable doubt as to the loyalty of the person involved to the Government of the United States.]

If mere words are to be believed this says that one is "guilty," *not* "innocent," if a reasonable doubt exists. The litmus test of loyalty is a travesty of American jurisprudence conveyed in gobbledygook. I think my mother was quite right to see that democratic government could not be separated from truthful, plain language. She passed off the McCarthy era as an aberration, as did many others, and retained her faith in the reasonableness of our political process. Reasonableness, in her case, ruled the decision of her Loyalty Review board and she was cleared and retained her job.

OPS folded in 1952, however, and until she married John DeWitt in 1956, she changed jobs and residence a good deal. With Johnny she had a good marriage and she was content. Her life entered a productive phase lasting nearly until his death in 1984. Johnny was a wiry, amusing, abrasive person of indomitable energy. He never lacked ideas for new projects. He shared with my mother a love of the written word and of the outdoors; of walks and dogs and dinner parties. In an age of the monorail career track, he was an exception, a generalist. He had studied chemistry in college, but in the late thirties he was writing two extremely successful and long-running radio serials. He served in the navy during the war, and afterward skippered a commercial fishing boat in Provincetown for a time. For the more than twenty-five years that he and my mother were married, he worked in Washington for government agencies as a public information officer. But at the same time, he actively remodeled a half-dozen houses in the city—he was a talented wood worker—and he collected and enjoyed good wines, played regularly and ruthlessly at his bridge club, and traveled widely.

Although Johnny was not an artist, he took a keen interest in the arts: music, theater and the plastic arts. His wood carving—while only a hobby, perhaps—produced over the years a large flock of exquisite birds fashioned from tropical hardwoods. But it was as an organizer that he made his contribution to the arts. Entirely on his own hook he convinced his superiors in the Department of the Interior that paintings, drawings and photographs are a useful and important medium of public information. Going on from there, as the first head of the Department's Visual Arts Program, Johnny commissioned working American artists to represent, as they would and at very little cost to the government, America's public lands, mainly in the West. Then, after cataloging the works that he had commissioned in the Department's name, Johnny mounted two shows of contemporary American landscape art. The second opened at the National Gallery of Art and coincided with the Bicentennial and both shows visited major museums of the country.

Johnny benefited my mother in many ways, but never more, I think, than connecting her practically as well as socially—through him and his work—to the contemporary American art scene and, once again, to the western landscape. He freed her from the necessity of working nine to five, and gave her time to return at last to her painting. And he gave her space to paint—a proper studio attached to their house in Washington. During her years in Washington she studied (with Bernice Cross, George Hamilton and Arthur Smith) and, I think, really developed as a painter. She showed and sold her work, which ignored the city and never ceased to contemplate the work of nature.

A very productive time ended when Johnny retired from government service and he and my mother went to Provincetown to live in a charming old house there. Thanks again to organizational efforts of Johnny's, this woodframe house had been moved to a beach location and had an attached studio. My mother painted a great deal in Provincetown, always learning, always refining. As she had done in Taos, she took her inspiration from what she saw in the natural world around her. It was in Provincetown, especially after Johnny's death, that her attachment to nature came to have also a full political expression.

The environmentalist's case is perhaps the most potent case against "development" and against the market system that can be made. My mother argued this case with vigor all through her last years. More sensible to mice, marshes and mountains than many people, she understood very well the environmental damage that had already been done to the Provincetown of her childhood and to the natural surroundings of her beloved Taos. There Blue Lake, near Taos and no longer sacred, was a venue for windsurfing regattas. There the slopes of a once-magic mountain were now cleared and groomed in winter for the convenience of skiers, old ground lower down replanted with their week-ender's condos. For summer fun a fabric balloon had been inflated on the valley floor. The giant mushroom housed a pair of tennis courts and al-lowed for air-conditioned play. Now it seemed that Taos Valley was no longer influencing its visitors, but very much the other way around. The visitors were importing a packaged life-style and their own air.

Time brought my mother many disappointments in her last years. Even before his death, Johnny DeWitt had put an end to their good and productive marriage. With each advancing year, old values were supplanted, old truths misrepresented, and old friends died away. Entering her ninth decade, she remarked that the eighties were not for sissies. At the same time, every day, like every new tide, brought her a sight, an item of interest to please her eye and buoy her spirits.

Her abiding interest in the natural world sus-tained her. That world had come to light in Taos. She had taken away a sensitivity to Nature and en-larged it. She once said that her two long-lived poo-dles, Rousseau and Meg, had assisted her further. Her pets had served her as animal guides had served the Indians. They had helped her to pierce the veil obscuring our ancient home.

I end with my mother's "Ode to a Sick Dog," written when Meg was seriously ill.

> Get well, Meggy
> Remember our walks
> In the woods
> On the dunes
> On the beach, on the flats.
>
> Remember the seagulls
> And especially
> Remember the sanderlings
> You chased
> Running along the verge
> With your high-pitched bark.
>
> Remember the good meals
> And the smelly delicacies you found
> Here and there
> Remember the vivid, bawdy tales
> Told by smells
> Along the streets.
>
> Remember Rousseau
> Who misses you
> And all of us
> Who love you
> And want you back.
>
> Keep up your courage, Meg
> Keep fighting
> Don't give up
> Life is good.